ROAD TO THE PYRENEES

ROGER HIGHAM

ROAD TO THE PYRENEES

WITH ILLUSTRATIONS BY THE AUTHOR
AND A MAP

LONDON
J. M. DENT & SONS LTD

Made in Great Britain
at the
Aldine Press · Letchworth · Herts
for
J. M. DENT & SONS LTD
Aldine House · Bedford Street · London

ISBN: 0 460 03907 5

To
MY WIFE, ISOBEL

CONTENTS

ILLUSTRATIONS

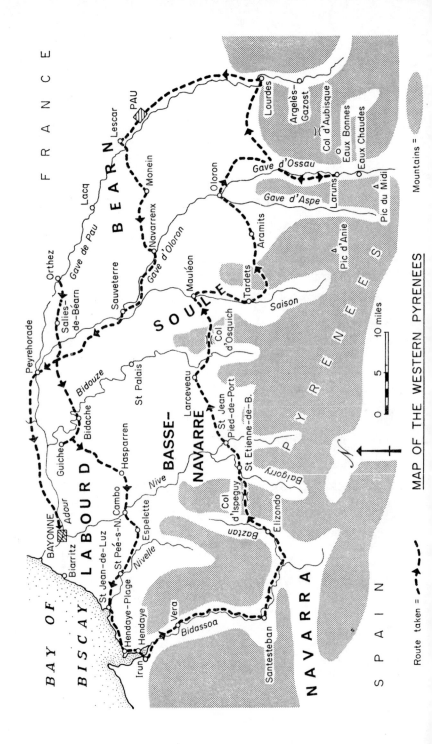

MAP OF THE WESTERN PYRENEES

Route taken = - - - ➤

Mountains =

Chapter One

THE NORTHERN MARCHES

The seats in second-class compartments of French trains are not remarkably comfortable: a long night's journey, sitting on one, could rate as a form of masochism. Sleep, if it comes at all, does so as a pleasant surprise.

I was quite glad of insomnia at half past five in the morning, however, because we were nearly in Bordeaux and the sun was rising. The sky was bright with its orange splendour, and the waters of the Garonne, as if the sun were Midas himself, had turned to molten gold. The full moon, which I had seen the evening before rising over Normandy, now was sinking into western Bordeaux.

'Good,' I thought, making a note on the first, clean page of my sheaf of paper, 'this will do to open the first chapter: "And by the time the train crept into the station of Bayonne, the sun was high, etc."'

After Dax the ticket collector came round. 'You cannot,' he said, looking at mine, 'go to Bayonne on this train. You will have to get out at Orthez and take the first train back.'

I remembered then that when I had boarded the train at Austerlitz station in Paris, the two coaches marked 'Bayonne' had been jammed full, so I had found a seat in the next one up; I could move down later, when there was more room. This necessity having escaped my memory during the long journey, I was now bound for Orthez.

Actually, it scarcely mattered. It meant changing my plans, but since I intended to visit Orthez anyway, in the course of the next few weeks' travels, I might just as well visit it now.

Once he had grasped that I was not trying to claim a refund on my ticket, the chap at Orthez station was very decent and refrained from charging an excess fare. The weather in Orthez was cool but sunny, and the first thing to do, after reviving my train-battered constitution with a cup of coffee, would be to find somewhere to put up for the night. Then I could begin walking the next day freshened by a good night's sleep.

I was equipped with the minimal necessities for camping: my old light tent, sleeping bag, groundsheet, some culinary equipment, a little solid fuel cooker that burnt tablets of some chemical substance, and a few spare clothes. All these were crammed into a travel-stained rucksack. I intended to follow my usual custom of walking for the greater part of the proposed distance.

Orthez, in common with almost the whole of the territory through which I wanted to travel, is in the Département of Basses-Pyrénées. The départements, administrative sub-divisions of France, were created soon after the Revolution, in 1790 to be exact, by the National Assembly. They dispensed 'for ever' with the old counties, viscounties, duchies and baronies, in the unquestioning assumption that every single Frenchman was heartily sick of them. In the case of Basses-Pyrénées, the two principal groups of inhabitants had never even considered themselves to be Frenchmen, and were therefore not in the least sick of them. The Basques and the Béarnais protested vigorously at being lumped together so arbitrarily. The Basques now had to accept the Béarnais capital, Pau, as theirs; the Béarnais must lose their Bishops of Oloron and Lescar and submit to the diocese of Bayonne.

And so perverse and independent are these numerically insignificant denizens of the South-West, that to this day, some hundred and eighty years after the Département was delineated, one hears very little of Basses-Pyrénées and a great deal about the Basque Country and Béarn.

The Viscounty of Béarn was created in the ninth century, which perhaps explains its inhabitants' resentment of the Revolutionaries' iconoclastic fervour. Orthez became its capital considerably later. The castle, which had probably existed in some form or another since Béarnais history began (and since there is virtually no written record of it until the eleventh century anything that happened prior to that date must be deduced or hazarded), was first constructed in recognizable form by Gaston VII, Count of Béarn. He built the tall, rhomboid keep, and called it Tour Moncade after his domains in Catalonia. Whereas his three Catalan predecessors paid more attention to the affairs of Spain than to those of Béarn, Gaston sold his lands in Catalonia and concentrated on Béarn. He transferred his capital from Morlaas to Orthez, but was obliged also to transfer his allegiance from Aragon to Gascony, whose dukes at the time happened to be the kings of England.

Gaston wanted Béarn to be an independent state, paying homage to no one; but those were inexorably feudal times. A spell of rebellious intrigue, of conniving with kings of Spain and France, was followed by a spell in prison at Winchester. After that, Gaston promised on behalf of his successors to be a faithful vassal.

Gaston VII built the Tour Moncade in 1242; another Gaston, a hundred years later, added two storeys to it. This was Gaston III of Foix. The recurrence of Gastons in Béarnais history is rather confusing, particularly as half way through their numbering stops and begins again. Gaston VII's daughter married a Count of Foix, and Counts of Foix had never been Gastons before, so there arose a situation similar to that of England and Scotland, where King James was First of one and Sixth of the other. Béarnais historians went on talking about Gastons VIII, IX, X and so on, and no doubt if they had had pillar boxes marked 'Gaston I' they would have blown them up.

The aforesaid Gaston III, both to single him out and to remove confusion with the previous Gaston III some hundreds of years earlier, was called Gaston Phoebus. He was a remarkable man and will reappear on the scene later in this narrative, but there is a rather sad story about him which was enacted in this castle at Orthez.

Gaston Phoebus had, for some time, been practising nepotism of the most blatant kind: his small circle of trusted administrators were recruited almost entirely from his own family, because these were the only administrators he could trust. The leading barons of Béarn, and the bishops of Lescar and Oloron, jealous of this system of government, corrupted Gaston's son and heir and induced him to conspire against his father. The plot collapsed, those conspirators who were unable to escape to Spain were executed, and the prince was imprisoned in

Orthez. Gaston, visiting him, tried to make him repent and return to his side; the boy refused either to speak or to take nourishment. After several equally profitless visits Gaston, for the last time, entreated his son to make amends. Weak from his hunger-strike, the boy said nothing. Losing his temper the Count thrust a dagger at his throat. Still the prince was silent. Gaston left in a fury; not a quarter of an hour later a desperate messenger came to him with the news that the boy was dead: the dagger had cut an artery, the boy had simply bled silently to death.

Having found a pleasant little hotel-restaurant in the Place d'Armes, the principal square of Orthez, and parked my baggage in the room, I ventured out to inspect the town. The castle was at the top both of my list of places to visit and of the town, which was built round the slopes of its steep hill. The sun shone benignly, and although there was a cool breeze there was warmth enough to sit on one of the benches near the castle and listen to the distant town-noises below. The castle was in pretty bad repair: not much was left of the curtain walls, only the tall, pale cream tower looked recognizably defensible. Even in the sunlight it appeared cheerless, and thinking of the fate of that obdurate youth made the breeze seem chillier.

Most of the town lay on the slopes of the hill between the castle and the river, the Gave de Pau. It was full of fascinating old houses, of all ages from the seventeenth century onward, and a few fragments of earlier date. Some houses had wooden balconies, some were of stone, some half-timbered, some had little odd towers. One, just down the road from the Place d'Armes, was apparently unchanged since the Middle Ages: all in stone like a castle, it was unpainted, unrepaired, but defiantly inhabited. In the courtyard of another, in Rue de l'Horloge, was the staircase turret and surviving fragment of Hôtel de la Lune, where the historian Froissart stayed in 1388.

Most of these delightful buildings were in good order, but one, which had better reason than most for preservation, was so decrepit that holes ventilated the roof and plants grew from the walls. This was the excellent renaissance house given by the town to Queen Jeanne d'Albret of Navarre. Béarn became part of Navarre in the late fifteenth century through the marriage of another count's heiress; having benefited greatly from the rule of King Henri II d'Albret, Béarn under Jeanne entered a period of religious wars. Jeanne was a Protestant, and tried to make everyone else follow her example. Since she was the queen this was quite easy: she simply made Catholicism illegal. She established at Orthez an Academy on the lines of Calvin's at Geneva, and obtained a majority in the Béarnais assembly, the States, for the enforcement of her doctrine. This provoked armed intervention from the King of France, and although his armies were defeated, the Béarnais, an easy-going race unaccustomed to associating religious differences with violence, suffered considerably from the excesses of the French soldiers.

When I had viewed this last house, the castle and the church, a tall, dark place, the morning was far advanced and I needed some lunch. I selected a bar from the many, persuaded the proprietor to make me a pâté sandwich, and enjoyed my first *pastis* on French soil for some years. An old man also taking nourishment in the bar addressed me in his thick South-Western accent, wanting to know if I was working in Orthez. My French, having enjoyed a prolonged vacation, was scarcely able to rise to a comprehensible reply, still less to understand every word the man said. There would be plenty of opportunity, subsequently, for it to improve.

After a jolly good snooze on my hotel bed I shook off the effects of the night's train journey and the *pastis*, and went down to the Gave to have a look at the old bridge. The new bridge was upstream, but still there were only the two of them, and the old bridge was too narrow for wheeled traffic. It was a stone bridge, of one large and three small spans, under which the Gave swirled muddily, and a tall tower half way across. It was built in the reign of Gaston Phoebus, in the fourteenth century, in order to facilitate the new trade-routes which were beginning to flourish under the guidance of that energetic ruler. Since it lay on the main route between Toulouse and Bayonne, and at the foot of one of the passes into Spain, Béarn became a commercial junction and its peasants, after centuries of wresting a penurious living from the unrewarding soil, found a lucrative alternative in the little workshops and factories in textiles, leather, metal and wood-work, and in the expanding export trade, all of which their count encouraged. At the beginning of the fifteenth century, this commercial endeavour having borne considerable fruit, the bridge at Orthez, this same bridge, received the right to charge tolls on certain specific merchandise which had to be carted across it en route to Bayonne.

One might well ask, if the bridge is too narrow for wheeled

The Old Bridge, Orthez

traffic now, and it was built specifically for increasing com-merce, was it not too narrow for wheeled traffic then also; and if so, why? Could the answer be that in the Middle Ages there was no wheeled traffic? Would the goods bound for Bayonne all have been strapped to the backs of horses and mules? The bridge is certainly wide enough for them.

Dinner at the hotel was good and inexpensive, and the Navarrenx wine was almost purple. The television in the bar showed an endless succession of politicians exhorting the populace to vote *oui* or *non* in the forthcoming referendum, which was based mostly on the decision whether to centralize or regionalize the country's government. The General, after eleven years in office, was facing a severe test of public confidence.

The first full day of my travels was Good Friday, but there was nothing very good about its weather, which declined to stop a persistent, depressing drizzle the whole day long. In the bar I sipped a cup of black coffee, watching the puddles, dripping trees and scurrying umbrellas in the Place d'Armes. The bill came to about thirty shillings, reasonable enough for a good bed and a good meal.

I crossed the Gave by the new bridge and made for the open country, which in brighter weather would have been wonderfully easy on the eye, consisting of small hills and valleys all wooded and farmed, rich in glowing spring-green verdure. The frequent farmhouses all had high, steep-pitched slate roofs, and the yards were as farmyards used to be before specialized, industrial farming set its dreary stamp on the land. Chickens, ducks and geese scratched about, the cattle byre was in the farmhouse, the untidy buildings exuded tradition and humanity. The lanes, even in the day's misty gloom, were cheered by their little hedgerow flowers, yellow, blue, white and pink; wild cherries, in full pink-and-white blossom, flowered in the woods.

An elderly, stocky farmer stopped his car and invited me to join him and his two dogs on the way to the village of l'Hôpital d'Orion. This weather, he said, was unusually bad for the time of year. He apologized for it, as if it were his fault.

The village was tiny. It had a little church and a comprehensive post-office-store-bar-restaurant; I confess that I visited the latter in preference to the former, but then it was still raining. With this inconvenient fact in mind, and having attended to my thirst, I began looking for some kind of shelter under which to have lunch. This, when on the road, usually consisted of fresh bread—half of what they call a *baguette*—and pâté or cheese, or both. Having failed to find anything remotely suitable I was, an hour later, only a couple of kilometres from

Salies-de-Béarn, my objective, when I saw a man standing in the doorway of a shed on a little rise by the roadside. He was holding a glass of something, and as I passed he lifted this and called to me, clearly inviting me to join him. I thought that with his permission the shed would make an ideal luncheon room, so mounted the rise and approached him. And I met Henri de Becque.

Henri was a man in his late fifties (so he told me later), but was still dark-haired; his eyes were bright, a clear grey-green, his nose was hooked, his face, clean-shaven, was tanned. One arm, the left, was tucked under his pullover in a sling.

'I saw you walking by,' he said, 'and thought you might like to join me in a glass of wine. It's my own wine, from my grapes that I grow here.' He pointed to the little vineyard which dipped and rose in the slight valley beyond the shed. Of course, he said, I could eat my lunch in the shed, and welcome.

'What,' I asked, 'have you done to your arm?'

'A motor accident, a month and a half ago. Smashed my car and broke my arm. It is hard, because I live on my own. My wife has gone away, my children have left home. But there is the good wine, thank God. Come, have some: it is perfectly natural, and does not affect the head.'

He went to a sack-covered cask in the gloomy interior of the shed and drew off some wine into a suspiciously grimy china jug. It was a rosé, light, cool, pleasant. As he refilled my glass, so I gave him more bread and pâté. He ate it so eagerly I suspected that his diet consisted more of 'the good wine' than anything more substantial. We finished the jugful of wine – 'if you too are alone, then you will find that the good wine is excellent for the morale, of which one has great need'—and we finished the bread and pâté.

'Come to my house,' said Henri, 'for a cup of coffee.'

He clapped on his head an incredible hat and led the way down the hill through the vineyard to his house, a small, single-storeyed cottage. 'It is very old, and not good.'

The main room, the kitchen, was filthy dirty and painfully sparsely furnished: a small wooden table, a wormy chair, another with no back; a black fireplace, dead ashes; a curly yellow calendar with a picture, from a wine merchant; a fly-blown bare electric light bulb; a bare, uncarpeted wooden floor. Henri turned up the butane gas stove and asked me to strike a match to light it; he found a spare cup, went outside to rinse it in the well, and dropped it. I heard him curse. He rummaged and found another, grey with dirt, and asked me to wash it this time. A couple of wipes with a cloth removed the worst of the grease, and Henri filled it and his own with hot black coffee. He offered me a cigarette. Normally I do not smoke, but on occasions such as these it is better to be sociable. It seems that whenever I do smoke, the cigarettes are always foully strong Gauloises, or Arab Supérieurs, or similarly poisonous breeds.

'The trouble is,' said Henri, 'that with my arm like this I can do so little. I cannot work, I cannot even clean the house, as you can see—and the days are so long, so very long. I become frustrated with boredom.' He gestured towards a wine bottle on the table filled with what I at first, not unnaturally, took to be white wine. 'So I take a little alcohol, both to kill the pain of my damned arm and to help my morale. Have some?'

What kind of alcohol it was, I have no idea: gin, rum, poteen, it could have been anything. I had finished most of my coffee by the time he poured some in my cup, so that what was left was cooled to sub-tepidity at once. It was strong as hell. I managed, like half of the second cigarette, to sling some of it out of the open door while Henri was not looking, but seeing I had an empty cup he promptly refilled it. He recommended dissolving some sugar in it, but that did little to improve its taste: it was ghastly.

The drizzle was still drifting mistily across the land when we emerged and climbed back up through the vineyard to the shed by the road. 'If you want a good, cheap hotel in Salies,' said Henri, 'try the Hôtel du Commerce, in a square on the left as you go into the town.'

I picked up my rucksack, which I had left in the shed, and swung it on to my back; I thanked Henri for his hospitality and hoped that his arm would soon get better so that at least he could pass the time more pleasantly.

'Monsieur,' he said, 'it is I who am grateful to you for coming to sit and talk with me. It is so seldom that I meet anyone: the neighbours are not kind and I am lonely. But I keep up my morale, as you do in your travels. One needs courage, does one not?'

One needs also to be almost permanently plastered, judging by the effect Henri's wine and 'alcohol' were beginning to have on me. I trotted blithely down into Salies and by some miracle found the Hôtel du Commerce, in its square, and it had a room. It was still raining, but instead of sensibly staying in and trying to dry off, I had the notion that I ought to do my duty and inspect the town, which was a ludicrously silly thing to do because having done so I lost my way entirely and spent hours trying to find it again. After two quite obviously wrong turnings I found the right one, more by luck than dead reckoning and sense of direction, staggered back to the hotel and collapsed on the bed until dinner.

The main course at dinner was fried *limande*, which my dictionary says is a dab or mud-fish. It was delicious. The wine was dark red and heavy, which with fish was contrary to accepted conventions, but just goes to show that the French might not be so fussy about what goes with what as some of us always assume they are. The wine, let me add, was simply placed on the table as a matter of course. It was perhaps a mistake on my part to have drunk anything stronger than Vichy water, because a very amiable conversation after dinner with a young man at the next table and the son of *la Patronne* could have been keenly interesting to relate, had I remembered a single word of it.

Feeling a good deal clearer in the morning, although instantly breakable, I had a good shave in hot water and felt better still. The morning, although still not particularly warm, was much brighter, with a soft wind and some sun. After leaving Hôtel du Commerce I paused in the gardens outside the Thermal Baths to adjust myself and find out from the map where I was supposed to be going. The Baths were in best Thermal Station rococo, with alternating courses of red and cream stone and little turrets at the corners; I have no information on the efficacy of their waters, but suppose they are influenced by the salt which has been found locally since Béarnais pre-history (the eleventh century, as previously remarked). Until the end of the Middle Ages (a vague era covering, as required, anything from four to eight hundred years; in this case until the sixteenth century) the salt of Salies was the only mineral exploited in all Béarn. The best story about it has a typically individualistic Béarnais flavour.

In the hope of putting an end to a contraband traffic in salt in the South-West, Louis XIV's minister Colbert authorized the confiscation of the salt springs of Salies. Thoroughly enraged, the Béarnais organized an open revolt, to such purpose that Colbert was obliged to come to terms with them. The compromise effected was that while the sale of salt was forbidden in most of the South-West, it was permitted in Béarn and the adjoining Basque provinces of Soule and Basse-Navarre. Even then, the royal agents for the collection of tax on the salt found themselves hedged on all sides by a populace unco-operative to a conspiratorial degree: when required to raise a statue in honour of the Sun King, the all-powerful Louis XIV, the Béarnais inscribed on its pediment the legend 'Here is the grandson of our Great Henri.'

By which of course they meant King Henri IV of France and Navarre, Béarn's contribution to the list of France's finest kings.

I found my way through streets of delightful old houses with flower-decked wooden balconies, crossed the stream and made for the open country again. This was flatter than yesterday's example, because it was the valley of the Gave d'Oloron. Farms were profuse and prosperous: huge barns, with steep Béarnais roofs and outbuildings attached on either side, like the arms of a man leaning on a table (or bar) with his hands outstretched. Often, the farmer's living quarters were to one side of the great arched central door. Most of these farms were constructed in the eighteenth century, when farming standards improved throughout the province and the old wood-and-mud houses were replaced by walls of stone from the riverbeds, roofed with slate from the mountains. In 1787 these new, substantial farm buildings surprised that early, observant tourist Arthur Young by their neatness and apparent wealth.

The quiet village of Carresse supplied me with bread and a glass of wine. On leaving it I passed a wonderfully decrepit and overgrown mansion, then crossed by an iron bridge the Gave d'Oloron, wide, shallow and rapid, with a canal-like backwater alongside, and entered the village of Auterrive. The houses here were quite different from those in Carresse, the simple action of crossing the Gave, the traditional frontier of Béarn, had the apparent effect of changing the style to that of the Basques: whitewash, patterns of painted wood, shallower roofs with deep overhanging eaves. This tendency was most marked in the village of Labastide-Villefranche, which stood on a hill overlooking the valley of the Gave, with an old stone tower at one end and a weird, elaborate Italianate palace in spacious grounds at the other. I passed an odd little corner turret belonging to this, then climbed the hill and inspected the former. With typical practical sense, the villagers had walled up the entrance to this picturesque but useless donjon and used the wall for a pelota court.

The houses in Labastide looked more solid than the old tower, as if they had been there as long. One, typical of all, declared itself a bar, so I went in. The great arched central doorway gave on to a tall barn-like hall, floored in concrete (but more than likely in beaten earth until recently), with a stove in the middle and a wooden staircase winding away up in the far end. Half a dozen men were sitting at a table, chatting and joking over a glass of wine; I followed their example and while the owner, a thin man in middle age, was pouring it, asked him about the Italianate palace.

'It is not old, that. A lady owns it, but she lives in Paris, and it is a kind of show-place, with gardens and cloisters for visitors. There used to be another tower there, and they say there is an underground passage from one to the other.'

'And how old is the tower?'

'Of the thirteenth century, Monsieur.' That was the time when several new villages, called *bastides*, were built for the benefit of the poor and unprotected populace.

The owner, noticing that I was obviously foreign, asked if I was German or English. I told him, and explained what I was doing in the South-West.

'Ah, yes,' he said, 'that is good. The more people know of each other's countries, the better they can understand each other. You know, Monsieur, we in Europe ought to work together for a common cause. We should tour, on holiday, in each other's countries, and play sports, and have done with wars and politics. We are all the same kind of people basically, and we could do so much better if we were united economically. Do you agree?'

Since France, represented by the General, had been the main obstacle to this ideal, and particularly to Britain's participation in it, this man's opinion surprised me. His wife and teenage son, a student on holiday for Easter, joined us. Since Madame was Basque I showed her a short glossary of Basque words I had brought from home; she corrected it in several instances, and eventually they allowed me to bring out my bread and cheese and pâté and eat it there, fortified by a second glass of wine.

After Labastide-Villefranche the road, a poor neglected Nationale, made for some wild uncultivated country. Having recovered from the shock of seeing that the splendidly arched and towered palace, cream-washed and set in lawns and trees and flowering shrubs, was called 'Le Bijou', I followed it, admiring the clusters of mistletoe that grew abundantly in the trees and the palms in the occasional cottage garden. The road was long and straight, and the weather was tending once more to be sulky. I came to Came, where there were a number of furniture-makers, craftsmen in carved wooden chairs with rush seats. It was just beginning to rain when a man in a car offered me a lift and I went with him to Bidache.

If it was going to rain all the evening, I did not want to camp; I mentioned this to the man in the car, a ruddy-faced, thick-set young fellow in the inevitable blue beret, and he volunteered to ask on my behalf at an inn in Bidache for a room. As it happened, the inn was full of *la jeunesse* who had descended on Bidache for Easter, and so was the other inn.

'I suggest,' said the man, 'that you come with me to my village, Guiche, which is not far from here and has a good inn. It is very pretty, and quite near the Adour, a most beautiful river.'

It was now raining quite heavily, so I thought this would be a good idea. On the way out of Bidache he pointed out the castle, which stood on a spur of rock overlooking another river, the Bidouze. It was ruinous but quite sizeable.

'There was once a battle here,' said the bucolic one.

'Oh? When, and between whom?'

'I don't know when: a long time ago. It was against the English.'

He drove along a winding, hilly road with fine views (in between the grey rain-clouds) of the lower Adour basin, towards Bayonne and the coast. Guiche, from the point of view of a walker, seemed to be a long way from Bidache, and I began to regret not having stayed to see the castle. However, gift horses must not be despised. My benefactor drove to Guiche, which was perched on top of a hill, and seeing someone he knew in the street, stopped and asked her if she had a room for me. She too, it seemed, was full of *la jeunesse*.

'We shall try another couple of places,' he said, 'down by the river. I will show you the great Adour.'

We descended to the river bank and drove along it as far as the confluence with the Bidouze. The water was yellow with mud, but one could see that in finer weather its beauty would be undeniable. 'You can walk all the way to Bayonne on the river bank. Why don't you try it?'

The two inns he mentioned were also full, the last at a part of Guiche built round a little castle on a smaller hill, called la Bourgade. 'There is one more chance,' he said, 'and after that I don't know.'

But at this last inn, in the main street of Guiche, there was room, and the young man, after chatting for a while with the owner, who was decorating part of it, departed, glad, he said, to have been able to help. The house was a huge place, haphazardly planned; my room also was huge, and lacking somewhat in furniture to cover the wide open spaces. But the people were charming and the dinner excellent, and after it I talked with the young son and daughter of the house, and their friends. They wanted to know about me, and when I said that I should move on in the morning, the son said: 'But if you go so soon you will be able to see nothing and say nothing of Guiche. Why not stay another day? Tomorrow is Easter anyway, and nothing will be open.'

This seemed reasonable. I could walk back to Bidache, perhaps, and look at the castle; and the inn was a good inn.

It was drizzling again in the morning; but there was no point in hanging about, so I took a narrow and circuitous country lane in the direction of Bidache, having announced that I should like to stay on. It was the wrong lane, and after wriggling about from farm to farm deposited me on the road along which the bucolic one had driven me yesterday. It was high, wide-open country, and as the rain cleared and the sky brightened, and I arrived at the top of one of the ridges of hills, suddenly I could see the Pyrenees. First there were the smaller heights, eastward by the coast, then the uncertain shapes of the great snow-covered mountains, emerging from

The Castle of Bidache

the clouds, shining briefly, one after another, then vanishing again.

It was sunny now, and peaceful; it was Easter, so there was no traffic as yet. A cuckoo piped up from the fresh green woods below the road, the faint tinkle of sheep-bells carried on the wind, a dog barked, a cock crew. I emerged from a tree-lined part of the road and saw the castle of Bidache standing on its knoll by the river. Dornford Yates, a novelist who knew and loved this country well, wrote:

'... Bidache itself gave us a château—ruined, desolate, and superb. There is a stateliness of which Death holds the patent: and then, again, Time can be kind to the dead. What Death had given, Time had magnified. Years had added to the grey walls a peace, a dignity, a charm, such as they never knew while they were kept. The grave beauty of the place was haunting.'

In the main street of Bidache there were houses which had rooms and galleries over an arcade, a paved refuge from sun and rain. One was dated 1661, but all looked venerable. I asked a policeman if the château was open to the public.

'Go and see the caretaker, Monsieur. He lives in the big house down yonder: you see the door?'

The house must have been the stables of the castle. I walked up the raked gravel drive, looked about, entered by the appointed door. The caretaker appeared, a charming, trembling old man, anxious to please, but 'unfortunately it is too early Monsieur. If you were to come back in the afternoon, when the crowds begin to come, you could join a party and I would guide you around the château. Come back at half past three, or four'.

I walked down the lane past the castle. It had a huge round tower and classical quarters of an early-renaissance appearance superimposed on it. All were crumbling, ivy-grown, battered, and home to rooks and pigeons. I lunched below the round tower, down by the river; before I had finished the low grey clouds started looming coldly from the west again and I suspected that today's ration of sunshine was now expended. I climbed back up to the town, called at a bar that had seen better days and at least more than the one customer, listened to the tale of woe of the old *patronne* who clearly shared the same characteristic as her establishment. I tried, unsuccessfully (naturally enough: I am no mechanic) to mend her sewing machine, and waited to see if the sun would reappear. It did not, and concluding that three hours would be too long to wait for the guided tour of the castle, set off back to Guiche.

I found the lane I should have taken in the morning, a beautifully rustic path through sparsely inhabited country, beside the Bidouze, a slow stream wide as the Medway at Maidstone. Half way to Guiche the rain started again, heavy showers developing into heavier and accompanied by thunder and lightning. I dodged between shelters of several kinds and managed to reach Guiche without getting too drenched.

The thunder was still rolling around an hour after I returned.

Guiche itself, which I saw for the first time properly during a brief sunny interval after the storm, was a tiny place built all on a ridge, with an offshoot round the little castle farther down by the river. The church of Guiche was huge in proportion to its couple of dozen houses, of warm cream stone, and had a charming colonnaded gateway with steps and a little room above.

Later, while I was having a drink in the inn's bar and a chat with Madame *la patronne*, who was a Basque, I had the luck to meet a little man in priest's collar and cassock, gold-rimmed spectacles and a black spade beard. He spoke English and said he was a missionary.

'I am trying,' he said, 'to write a book on Guiche; but time is so short, and soon I have to go to Formosa.'

'Do you know,' I asked, 'anything about a battle which is supposed once to have been fought near here?'

'Yes, it wasn't a very important affair, actually. It came at the end of the Hundred Years' War, when the English lost control of Gascony. This is part of Gascony, you know: it is neither Béarn nor Basque Country, although like Madame here there are several Basques around. People still speak Gascon.'

'What's that, a dialect?'

'It's really a language on its own. You've heard of the Langue d'Oc? It's a dialect of that.' No wonder the conversation of the worthies in for a red-wine session was so difficult to understand.

He told me about pelota, the national game of the Basques, and some of the eighteen different ways of playing it: outdoors, in the fronton, the wall and court; indoors in the trinquet court; with bare hand, with glove, with chistera (the curved claw-like basket attached to the hand). I could have kept asking him questions all night, but he had to go.

Chapter Two

LABOURD

The inn at Guiche, as I have observed, was a good inn. It had, perhaps, its shortcomings in the matter of superficial comforts, like the curious angle of the mattress and the uncertainty of the hot water; but in things that really count it was unimpeachable. My second dinner there was the more memorable. There was some lamb, so young and tender I thought at first it was a species of fowl as yet unknown to me, and there was some Bayonne ham and peas, and some strong, pale cheese that Madame had made herself. And of course, the good red wine. And the whole thing, as I discovered in the morning, was almost absurdly inexpensive. 'Things in the country,' said Madame, 'are not as dear as they are in the towns.'

The morning was quite promising; I left Guiche and took that high, dipping road from which it was today impossible to see the Pyrenees, to Bardos, where I stocked up with supplies. With a bit of luck the weather would stay fine for camping that night. Camping was unavoidable in any case, because it was Easter Monday; no banks would be open, and I had not enough money for even the humblest of inns.

From Bardos onwards I was within the vaguely defined bounds of the Basque Country. Sir Winston Churchill once said of predicting the actions of Russia that 'it is a riddle wrapped in a mystery inside an enigma.' One might well say the same thing of the origins of the Basques.

The Basques are quite definitely a distinct race, ethnically and linguistically, and the really curious thing is that although large numbers of them, over the centuries, have emigrated, their homeland has remained since pre-history in exactly the same place, astride the Pyrenees. That in itself is odd, for the great mountain chain is an obvious natural barrier. Although for many centuries this barrier has divided

them into French Basques and Spanish Basques, yet they have
preserved their identity and their language, as separate and
distinct as if they had been an independent nation all this
time. M. Henri Pouy, writing in a French railway magazine,
says that they are 'a race adventurous and virile, proud and
stern, simple and friendly, the faithful guardian of traditions
whose origin has long been lost in the mists of time, but who
still appear, in the eyes of travellers, to be somewhat mysterious
and distant'.

Because of this touch of the mysterious, the Basques have
been the subject of endless speculation and discussion, some
of which, to help add to (or perhaps even reduce) the reader's
confusion, I shall introduce in the course of this narrative.

There are altogether seven Basque provinces, four in Spain
and three in France. The one whose borders I was now
approaching was Labourd, the westernmost in France. The
country was hilly, green and pretty without being remarkably
spectacular, and reminded me somewhat of the Kentish Weald.
The sun lasted long enough for my wayside lunch, but deserted
when I reached Labastide-Clairence, a village on a hillside
whose main street was full of text-book Labourdin houses, all
deep-eaved, solid and white-washed, many with overhanging
storeys, and of all ages from the sixteenth century onwards,
according to the dates which the builders had all obligingly
written above the door. I stopped for a drink in the Hôtel
Trinquet, named after its court for indoor pelota, stayed long
enough for the rain to get well established again, and left
while it was still splashing determinedly down. Fortunately,
quite soon after I left the village, a young man offered me a
lift to Hasparren and I accepted with enthusiasm. I asked
him if there was an official camping site in or near the town,
and he was sure there was, but not where it was. Nor was
anyone else I asked. 'One climbs up the little lane. But wait—
perhaps it is not yet open.'

One climbed up the lane, which was about one in three,
and arrived breathless at the road, which had negotiated the
gradient more sensibly in a series of bends. There was no sign
of the official 'Camping', but there was the hill, covered in
woods and devoid of fences, up which I had just laboured. I
ventured up one of its paths, past one or two large stone

Houses in Espelette

crosses, and emerged from the trees at a little shelf below
another cross. Beyond it, at the crest of the hill, were three
more: a Calvary. As I was unpacking and pitching my tent
(it had stopped raining during the car ride into Hasparren)
three nuns came walking up the path, evidently making for
the crosses. I greeted them.

'Is it all right if I camp here?'

'Certainly, Monsieur. What a fine view you will have!'

The good lady was absolutely right; I had been so busy
fussing with my gear that I had not noticed it. The view
started with the whole of Hasparren, at the foot of my hill,
spread to a blanket of green hills and valleys, white-flecked
with farmhouses, and extended to a dim blue distance.

My camp properly established, and after a comparatively
brief shower, I went down the violently steep little lane into
the town. It was full of young people of both sexes milling
around and café-crawling, and a funeral procession was just
emerging from the church. A notice pointed to a 'Roman
stone' behind the church, and this turned out to be an inscribed
tablet set up in a nicely curved new stone terrace. A note, in a
glass case, accompanied it, translating the Latin words (which
ran into each other in that exasperating Roman fashion) into
French. Here is a translation of them into English:

'The priest Verus, duumvir, quaestor, president of the
district, going in deputation to Augustus, has obtained the
separation of the Nine Peoples from the Gauls. On his return
from Rome, he dedicated this tablet to the people of this
place.'

This brings us to an anomaly: Hasparren, where this tablet
was discovered (in the sixteenth century), is in Labourd, a
province of the Basque Country. Yet Hilaire Belloc, in his
classic text-book *The Pyrenees*, says that 'the Basques themselves
are not known to us from the Romans'.

The Nine Peoples, whose delegate to Rome, Verus, managed to obtain separation for them from the rest of Gaul,
occupied all the territory from the Garonne to the Pyrenees.
If we know nothing from the Romans of the Basques, then we
know precious little of the others either, except for their names,
particles of which survive here and there. From east to west
of this area, there came first the Consevanni (Conserans),

then the Convenae (Comminges), the Bigerriones (Bigorre), the Benarnensii (Béarn), the Elloronensii (Oloron), the Auscians and the Tarbelli, centred at Dax, which latter were subdivided into three, thus making up the nine. The Tarbelli and the Auscians seem to have occupied the Basque Country north of the Pyrenees, so presumably these were the Basques themselves. Belloc surmises that 'the silent strength of the Basques prevented the Roman language from invading their valleys'. There is evidence of Basque-type place names over the whole of this area—a fact which has set ethnologists and philologists at odds for generations—but there is so little real evidence of who the Nine Peoples actually were that one can only guess.

At all events, they appear to have been as independent-minded under the Romans as they have been ever since, judging by the evidence of this tablet in Hasparren, which dates from the late third century A.D., when the Nine Peoples wanted to be a distinct autonomous province, apart from Gaul, and free from Gaul's scale of taxes. All Verus achieved was to separate them administratively, but it seems that about two hundred years later, in the declining imperial years, they did gain their complete independence.

The name Hasparren is derived from Haitza-barren, the valley of oaks; but although some oaks survive on the Calvary hill on which I had camped, nothing was left of such a forest justifying the name. After filling my water-can (a plastic thing bought in Mateur, in Tunisia, some years before) from the fountain in the square, and myself with a couple of glasses of wine from a bar in a side-street off it, I climbed back up that precipitous lane and the hill-paths, past the crosses, to my eyrie. Getting ready for supper I discovered that I had been joined by a large colony of ants which was feasting on a quantity of marmalade which had spilled from its plastic container into a rucksack pocket. I also found that my im-provised handle for a tin in which I proposed to boil water for coffee and washing-up (my old billy-can having become inexplicably lost) was a total failure: it spilt half the water. I had decided not to cook, and supper, a rather disgruntled affair, was really a repetition of lunch, sustaining but not very exciting. Afterward I lit a candle and read for a while, becoming conscious gradually of three separate factors: one, that the town youths were making an almighty racket with their yelling and singing way down below; two, that it was going to be uncomfortably cold; and three, that my weight-saving measure of doing without an inflatable rubber mattress or airbed was going to make the night a long one.

Considering all these things, that the Easter Monday yahoo went on until the early hours, that it had been indeed very cold, and that the ground was hard and uneven, I had quite a good night and even slept. It was either the church clock striking the hour or the screaming of pigs that woke me; pigs always scream whether they are being fed or slaughtered, and I hoped it was the former. It turned out to be neither: there was a market in full cacophonous spate when I got down to the town, and the pigs, in common with every other kind of domestic animal imaginable, were being simply pushed around. Even humans sometimes scream when that happens. The town, whose squares and streets were packed with stalls selling commodities as varied as the aforesaid creatures, was jammed full of farmers and their wives, the former concerned with the creatures, the latter with the commodities. All transactions, in either form of merchandise, entailed the absolute maximum noise: the sale of a kilo of apples was clearly quite impossible without the kind of voice-production normally reserved either for R.A.D.A. students or for hailing ships at sea. The farmers, all equipped with the universal blue beret as if it had grown there instead of hair, were all short, square and red-faced; whether they spoke in a patois or in Basque was difficult to say, since they did so all at once and in this manic shout. In any case, the effect was of splendid animation.

When I had refilled my wallet (after waiting in the bank behind a number of these rectangular, bereted farmers) and despatched cards and letters at the post office, I left town on the road to Cambo. I followed a lush green valley, past an eroded old castle on a hill like mine of the Calvary. Shortly after I had plodded up a steep hill I was offered a lift, and a few minutes later was standing in Cambo-les-Bains.

The full name of this town, and the reason for its existence, were provided by the springs of sulphurous water which ensured that in the era when such places were popular, it became a Thermal Station. Around the bath-house were built a number of large, ornate villas in that rococo style indispensable to Thermal Stations, all on the high hill overlooking the valley of the Nive. The original Cambo, a village of fine old Basque houses, still stands in the valley, on the other side of the river. The sulphurous waters are no longer exploited; but Cambo is still a popular tourist centre because the fancy villas were large enough to turn into hotels and the town's situation made it ideal as a centre for viewing Labourd, Basse-Navarre and the mountains. The inevitable adjunct of tourist centres, the souvenir shop, thrives on the sale of its multifarious, useless, repellent and spurious articles. Bars are numerous and characterless. The best thing about the place is the view of the shining, rapid Nive, old Cambo and the green hills behind it, and the railway sidings. I visited the church. It was typical of what I had heard of Basque churches: a high apse-less nave, brightly painted, with three carved wooden galleries around the western end, one above another, intended for the men; segregation of the sexes being considered proper, the women were allowed the floor.

Mistaking the way out of Cambo, I returned to a cross-roads café where the lads were feeding coins into a juke-box to hear a tune that had been popular in England some three months previously, the cleaned-up version of an old Rugby-club type of song called 'Lily the Pink'. The French version, I am glad to say, did it full justice.

I entered the village of Espelette at about two in the afternoon (it had not rained quite so much so far), and so admired it that I decided to find an inn and stay the night. Some Basque cooking, I thought, would not come amiss at this juncture. The inn I chose was in a back street, a little corner just behind the main thoroughfare. It was a typically vast wooden place in the local style, and the resident family were undeniably Basque: I heard the owner conversing in it with two fellows in for a drink.

Espelette stands on a hill above a stream which contributes to the Nive; it is surrounded by hills and the larger foothills of the mountains, peaks which have names such as Ereby, Mondarrain and Artzamendi (which means Bear Mountain), all of which are as bright in their verdure as any in Ireland.

Espelette

The village consists of a text-book display of examples of
Basque domestic architecture, and rejoices in the achievement
of having twice won the title Prettiest Village of France. The
Mairie is in a very old house attached to an even older defence
tower, on a prominence overlooking the stream. The last time

the Prettiest Village diploma was won was in 1955, since when, judging by the state of the Mairie, Espelette has not tried so hard.

While I was sketching the church from a point near the fronton, in which several small boys were practising their pelota, I happened to leave my rubber on the nearby wall. I realized this when I began a second drawing, higher up in the village, and returned for it. As I approached the fronton one of the diminutive pelota players came towards me with the rubber in his hand, and gave it to me. I thanked him: tongue-tied, he just grinned and ran home.

Dinner—vegetable soup, an omelette of herbs and a cutlet of veal—was good but not particularly Basque in character. I ate it alone in the cavernous bar-cum-dining-room that ran the length of the ground floor of the house; the people of the house, although polite, were not communicative. But the bed was excellent, the bill was not high and the morning was the best yet. I left Espelette on the way to St Jean-de-Luz in bright sunshine through delightfully pretty valleys and hills, the hedgerows gay with primroses and violets, the birds singing, the cow- and sheep-bells tinkling, and a little soft breeze to temper the heat.

I came to a village called Souraïde which was so fresh painted and immaculate that it appeared brand new. Which, on closer inspection, most of it was: lots for building had been sold, but the houses were still the vast, square, deep bastions in the exact tradition. The Mairie, *Herriko Etchea* in Basque, which means People's House, was dated 1965, but its style was that of some I had seen dated 1765.

The hillsides and the valley bottoms were divided into small fields and pastures, and there were numerous farmhouses, aged buildings with living quarters, cows, machinery and hay all under one roof. With a thin and unproductive soil, there could never be a wide range of cultures in the Basque Country; but the grass is always green, so the tradition is of sheep and cattle grazing. With so many small holdings it might be thought that no one could make a decent living, but in fact the crux of the Basques' rural society has been, from earliest times, that they have maintained a collective policy. The house is the nucleus of the society, symbolizing the family. Most

Basque names are taken from the patrimonial house; among the most common are *Etcheberry*, 'new house', *Etchegaray*, 'hillside house', *Larramendi*, 'mountain-side'. The houses, which are nearly always orientated to face east or south, are capable of extension to accommodate new members of the family, and are always inherited by the eldest son. The younger children, having little to do and being also a burden on the farm's capabilities, are prone to emigrate; in fact emigration is practically an industry with the Basques. But although the junior members of the family go to North and South America in large numbers every year, and often make good through their skills in shepherding and pasturage, they maintain their links with home, send money to support the farm and frequently return to the family house in old age to live in retirement.

The tradition for managing their meagre lands communally saved the Basques from the atrocious exploitation of the peasant, 'Jacques Bonhomme', which characterized the rest of France until the Revolution. Mediaeval feudalism was almost unknown to them, and the power of the monarchy was limited. Even the Kingdom of Navarre, the Basques' own monarchy, curtailed the privileges of aristocracy and clergy—foreign aristocracy that is, the Basques had none of their own—and ensured that individual interests were subordinated to those of the family house, and those of the house to those of the community.

Farming methods were and are primitive, because the diminutive size of the properties makes modernization difficult. Oxen are still used more than tractors, and milking machines are unknown. Flocks of two or three hundred sheep are usual, and the ewes are milked for the making of cheese. But the pastures are always green, and the communal lands, managed by syndicates of the house-masters—*etcheko jaun*—ensure that a reasonable degree of prosperity is possible. Life is never easy, and the Basque farmer is seldom affluent, but the Commune protects him from penury.

From the top of a col, a saddle in the hills, near a noisy, grey grit quarry, I caught a glimpse of the sea. A long, gentle, easy and pleasant descent through woods and fields brought me to the valley of the Nivelle and the village of Saint-Pée-sur-Nivelle, guarded by a tumbledown old keep.

This tower, which was built in 1403, was two hundred years later the scene of one of those bouts of superstitious savagery which now and then blacken the human race: there was a witch-hunt, and many unfortunate women were burnt to death, without proper trial. More would have suffered but for the intervention of the Bishop of Bayonne, one Bertrand

Farmhouse near Saint-Pée-sur-Nivelle

d'Echaux, who had benefited from the approval of King Henri IV and arrived just in time to stop further burnings— but too late to save those already burnt.

Saint-Pée was another village totally Basque in architecture, character and flavour. The inn in which I chose to refresh myself, without being in the least self-consciously *touristique*, was a classic. The tables in the big room were bright with red

cloths patterned in the local fashion; a wooden staircase led
up to the next floor; and in the opposite corner was a fireplace
large enough to roast a sheep. Huge logs from last night still
smouldered on their massive andirons; the cosy inglenook
seats spoke plainly of the old men who had occupied them with
pipe, glass of wine and endless reminiscence; the mantelshelf
bore a gleaming regiment of brass candlesticks and pots. From
the dark, cavernous chimney itself there hung, mysteriously, a
great black hook: the stew-pot only was missing. *La Patronne*,
gold-toothed, cheerful, and in proportion with the fireplace
immense, told me that I had missed, by a day or two, the
fair at Espelette. Never mind, I said, I saw the one at
Hasparren.

'If you are going to Saint-Jean-de-Luz', she said, 'on no
account go by the main road. There is a much prettier road
through the forest, where there is the fine villa of a film actor.
Also it is shorter, by at least two kilometres.'

'Is he often at home, the film star?'

'No, mostly he is away, in Paris. His wife and mother live
there.'

She was perfectly justified in recommending the forest route;
it was lovely. I found the road quite easily after lunching on
the banks of the shining Nivelle, watching the fish jumping,
plopping in little concentric pools. It was hilly country, but the
valleys were full of greenwood, little streams and rustic magic,
and from the hill tops there were brilliant views of other hills
and valleys, of the far sea, of the mountains. The nearest
mountain was a wide but not spectacularly high prominence,
viewed sideways in the shape of a cheese-dish, called
La Rhune, which really is Larre-on and means Good
Moor: clearly a place where sheep could safely be left to
graze.

The film star's house was indeed a thing of splendour, but
a covey of bellowing Alsatians dissuaded me from spending too
long admiring it. In common with two or three other large
houses on this quiet road, it stood on a hill top and commanded
one of the views I have just mentioned. The woods were full
of tall, stately trees, cuckoos, and tree-top platforms which
puzzled me somewhat. Explanation came some while later.

I arrived after a warm climb in the suburbs—the railway

suburbs—of Saint-Jean-de-Luz, at the Nationale 10, and
sought irrigation and information at the nearest bar. The
weather now being obviously set fair and warm, I thought I
would camp, and further that the best place in which to do
this would be one of the several official camping sites near the
town. The lady in the bar, with even more gold teeth than the
one at Saint-Pée, recommended Camping Iratzia as the best
of them, and there I went, a kilometre or so from the town. It
consisted of a fine open, grassy field, quite near the sea—and
the road, and the railway. But never mind; it had a wash-
place and a row of those traumatic hole-in-the-ground lava-
tories, but as the season had not yet properly begun there
was no water connected with any of them. Nor was there
anyone around to collect fees. The only other occupant of the
field, a man with his family, tent and caravan, and I fetched
our water from a standpipe at the edge of the field and had it
to ourselves. The sun shone, my neighbour's little girls played
in the field, and I had a dhobey session, afterwards draping
socks and pants and handkerchiefs about the wash-sink nearest
to me, to dry in the sun and wind.

I walked the mile or two into town in the evening, to find
a restaurant and have dinner. I wandered around the darken-
ing streets of weathered old houses, watched from the *plage*
the setting sun casting its dazzling beam across the quiet
waters of the harbour, and selected from the many a restaurant
with an appetizing menu. If mussels are on a menu I can
seldom resist them; these were *à Jerez*, which meant that they
were cooked in sherry. *Poulet Basquaise* was roast, with thick
piquant sauce of tomato and red peppers, and rice. There
were only four other customers at the Hôtel Mazarin that
evening, and after our meal we gathered at one end of the
long empty room and chatted. The owners were Basque, with
the characteristic long, narrow face, black hair and hooked
nose. I asked Madame if she spoke Basque.

'Oh yes, we of my generation speak it, but very few of our
children do. Radio, television and newspapers are all in
French, you see, and our own language, which is very, very
difficult in any case, becomes an encumbrance.'

'Then it will die out. Would you not think that a great
shame?'

'Yes, a pity. But to be a Basque goes deeper than our customs and language: even our children realize that, so we remain violently nationalistic. But, you know, Monsieur, we are not aggressive, and I believe that many people in Europe feel more tolerant these days towards one another. Travellers come here, all kinds: you're English, good; you're German, good; you're Spanish, good. All are Europeans, are they not? All are basically the same. I think we should be a great *commune*, all of us, be at peace and become prosperous.'

The *patron* was telling the others of his grotesque experiences while mining for uranium in Bolivia. The mine was under an active volcano, and despite protective clothing and a ventilation system, it was so hot that only a few hours work per shift were possible; the walls of the mine were untouchable and it was commonplace for miners coming to the surface to faint and sometimes even die.

The walk back to the camp was cooler: the grass of the field and the walls of my tent were drenched with dew. As if to reinforce this there was a cold sea-mist during the night, which saturated the tent inside and out. Also, my old sleeping-bag, which had been nibbled by mice while in storage over the past year or so, now sprang several leaks and covered me with more feathers than a chicken-plucker. The morning, too, was obstinately cloudy, permitting no chance of drying out. I was, in the immortal words of Wodehouse, very far from being gruntled. I rose and packed the tent, which was wetter than when it had been rained on, and trudged into town. Camping, I was beginning to consider, was in these conditions so hellishly uncomfortable that it would have to be relegated to the status of an expedient of last resource, to be practised only when unavoidable. I should have to stay at inns, and because my pecuniary resources were not unlimited I should have to clip a week off my planned route in order not to finish it flat broke.

In Saint-Jean-de-Luz I searched for the post office, which had moved, found there were no letters for me, and went and had a beer in the appropriately named 'Bar de la Consolation'. Another one was that the sun was breaking through, and life at once began again to appear supportable. I went down to the inner harbour, a basin made by the mouth of the Nivelle before it reaches the sea; some fishing boats, small sturdy craft painted bright blue, were unloading their catch at the quay-side. The sailors, in berets and oilskin overalls, were boxing the fish and sluicing the scales off their decks. Hard as nails, the sailors, short, strong-bodied, faces like walnuts, were shouting and laughing in their own language, Labourdin Basque. They were the modern representatives of a race of mariners going back to Noah.

Saint-Jean-de-Luz was originally called by its Basque name, Donibane Loretzun. It had been the haven and home port of fishermen, whalers and pirates since pre-history. In their search for the whale and for cod, the Basque seamen reached the shores of America hundreds of years before the time of Columbus. In the thirteenth and fourteenth centuries they penetrated Hudson's Bay, sailed up the Saint Lawrence and along the coasts of Labrador, Greenland and Spitzbergen. In 1412 their whaling fleet operated off Greenland. Their mariners were in the forefront of every voyage of exploration: one piloted Columbus to Hispaniola, another, Juan Sebastian Elcano, was Magellan's second-in-command on his circum-navigation and took command when Magellan died.

As long as whales frequented the Bay of Biscay in the spring and autumnal equinoxes, Saint-Jean-de-Luz remained the greatest whaling port in the world. The kings of France allowed all manner of privileges to the Basque sailors because they supplied all Europe with the greater part of its whale produce—the essential oil, fat and grease that had not then evolved minerally. Fishing rights, granted direct from the king, were confirmed in periods of six to nine years, until Louis XIV, perhaps in recognition of having been married there (a restaurant in the town rejoices in the cumbersome name of Café Mariage de Louis XIV) extended this grant to thirty years at a stretch.

The prosperity of the port waxed most strongly from the thirteenth to the seventeenth century. By the end of the sixteenth century, the whaling fleet consisted of 80–100 ships of 200–300 tons, each crewed by fifty or more men. Around 3,000 sailors left the port each spring to go whaling and cod fishing. The whales, of course, eventually got the message and declined to visit the Bay of Biscay any more, which meant

that the fleet had to go farther to catch them. Then, between
1670 and 1796, there was a series of mighty storms, which
gradually destroyed the defence works and successively flooded
the town. Furthermore, the old fishing grounds of Canada and
Newfoundland (whose old name was Port-au-Basques) were
lost when the Treaty of Utrecht ceded them to Britain, and
the ships began to be requisitioned by the government for
naval service. As the town's prosperity declined, so did its
population: from nearly 14,000 in 1730, it had fallen to 3,500
by 1821. The Revolution, which in general was not approved
by Basques and Béarnais, did little to help: for two uncomfortable years it changed the town's name to Chauvin-le-
Dragon, and that of the square, Place Louis XIV, to Place
de la Liberté. It is now Place Louis XIV again, but you can
still see, on the wall below the left hand tower of Maison
Lohobiague, next to the Mairie, the faint letters of 'Place de
la Liberté'. When the Duke of Wellington and his army
arrived (and took up quarters in the town, Rue Mazarin)
the Basques received them with enthusiasm as liberators,
preferring an English occupation (unique among invading
armies, the English always paid their bills) to Napoleonic
imperialism.

The rebuilding of the harbour, after plans made by Vauban
generations before, was begun in 1836 but not finished until
fifty years later. Moles were projected from Socoa and Sainte-
Barbe, either side of the bay, and another, Artha, was built
in the middle. Steam boats arrived, and the fishing industry
picked up again. Now there are a hundred boats, fifteen
hundred sailors and a big service-vessel for tuna fishing, which
takes the boats as far as the coasts of Africa. They fish for the
tuna from May to October, for the sardine from October to
February, and for the anchovy from March to May. Since it
was now April, the boxes full of little silver fish, which were
being heaved dexterously on to trucks on the quayside, would
be of anchovies.

At the head of the harbour I crossed a bridge over the
Nivelle and went to Ciboure, a sister-town on the other side.
Ciboure's history (the name, in Basque, means 'head of the
bridge') runs parallel to that of Saint-Jean-de-Luz, but always
it preserved its identity and there was the inevitable rivalry

between sailors of the two towns. One curiosity of Ciboure was the existence of a colony of social outcasts called Cagots. This mysterious race once dwelt in odd spots all along the Pyrenees; they lived apart, they had no lands to cultivate and so made a living as wood-cutters, masons or weavers, and were abominated as accursed. Marriage with one was punishable by the ordinary Basque community with death. Clearly, since they could not intermarry, they eventually became extinct. There is no definite proof, but it is probable that they were the descendants of lepers.

I started to climb the hill by the waterfront, past the old house where the composer Maurice Ravel was born, and stopped for lunch at a little belvedere with a huge statue of the Blessed Virgin for the protection of sailors from the perils of their profession. I ate a couple of alleged pastiza cakes, the *vrai gâteau Basque*; but I think they must have been mass produced, they were poor things, no more than lemon curd tarts. I sat in the sun on the warm stone seat, watched suspiciously by a lizard, and surveyed the whole harbour from Socoa to Sainte-Barbe. Just then the only things afloat on it were little pleasure-sailing-boats, but one could see that without any difficulty it could accommodate an old-fashioned fleet of battleships.

I started the long trek out to the coast road, the *Corniche Basque*, through the straggling seaside villas of Socoa, past the road leading to the watch-tower and the yacht club, to the high cliffs where the mighty Atlantic roared and crashed thunderously on the rocks. No wonder I had thought they really were thunder last night, and had stayed awake for hours. For some curious reason, by this time my left ankle had developed an inflamed tendon, or some such anatomical structure, and was becoming increasingly painful. I assumed that in due course it would mend, and pressed on; but it made progress, already a bit of an effort under the hot sun with no shade, that much more problematical. The coast climbed and dipped at the whim of the cliff contours, and habitation was limited to one or two farmhouses, farther inland, countless camping sites and a huge holiday centre for railwaymen, which I first took to be a five-star hotel. The sea was blue, a pleasant, reasonable blue, unlike the indecent, overdeveloped

violet of the Mediterranean, and there was a breeze to mitigate
the heat.

I limped into Hendaye Plage, which was still asleep from
hibernation, and could see the Cabo Higuer, Cap du Figuier
or Cape of Figs, whichever you prefer, an arm of Spain reaching out into the Bay of Biscay. At Hendaye Plage I met a
fellow English vagabond whom I had last seen thumbing
traffic in Socoa. He arrived in a car, but said he had had to
walk half way here before anyone stopped for him. 'Oh,
well,' I said in tones of the most shameless *savoir-faire*, 'it's a
coast road; people never stop on roads like that. I never even
bother to try hitching.' It had not actually occurred to me
that I might do so, but the words were nevertheless true: past
experience had taught me that the faster and more riviera-like
the road, the less likely was a hitch-hiker to progress.

We parted at a roundabout with palm trees in the middle,
as he tramped off to the frontier—'I want to get to Bilbao
tonight'—and I collapsed in a pavement-café chair and poured
some cold beer down my throat. I wanted to get to Irún that
night, only just over the frontier, on my own two—well, one
and a half—feet. Refreshed and rested, I left Hendaye Plage,
skirting the mud-flats of the Bidassoa estuary, with Fuen-
terrabia towered and misty on the far side and boats lying at
unboatlike angles, and crept into Hendaye itself.

A typical frontier town, Hendaye was mostly built around
a priory and chapel on the pilgrim route to Santiago de
Compostela. There were several of these routes, and since we
shall come to another in due course I will say no more about
them at this point. Had I not been feeling at the time dis-
inclined to undertake any more walking than was necessary
to get to Spain, I should have gone to Rue de Santiago in the
town, because a priory in the street was at one time occupied
by the last surviving pirate of Hendaye. When the whaling
industry of the Bay of Biscay declined, many of the sailors took
to piracy; this one, Etienne Pellot by name, was nearly a
hundred years old in 1813 and was the only remaining
inhabitant of Hendaye to greet Wellington when he crossed
the Bidassoa, in recognition of which the Duke stayed as a
guest in his house.

An endless road, full of hotels and boarding-houses, banks

and money-shops, took me to the bridge across the Bidassoa and the frontier of Spain. My passport stamped, I entered a little glass hutch called Banco de España and changed a traveller's cheque. Pocketing the brown paper pesetas, I uttered my first words in Spanish to a Spaniard.

' *Muchas gracias.*'

'Don't mention it,' he said.

Chapter Three

BIDASSOA AND BAZTAN

Just inside the border, on the long road up to Irún, there was a souvenir shop with rows of new yellow gourds hanging outside. When Hilaire Belloc wrote *The Pyrenees*, some sixty years ago, the gourd was the best thing possible for carrying one's liquid necessities on a walking and climbing expedition. But, warned Belloc, 'if you can get an old gourd second-hand that does not leak, it is far preferable to a new one; all things really worth having are better old than new.' He would certainly not have approved of these meretricious objects, probably manufactured with a view to sale to tourists, who would undoubtedly hang them up on a wall rather than drink out of them. In point of fact, drinking out of them requires a good deal of skill, because one has to 'grasp with your right [hand] the bottom of the leather bottle; tilt the whole up, squeeze slightly with your right hand, held high in the air, and let the thin straight stream of wine from the little hole go straight into your open mouth; then (to paraphrase Talleyrand's famous phrase to the Maker of Religions), "if you can possibly manage it", let it go down without swallowing; if you swallow you are lost.' That is not all: there are further problems, the mastery of which distinguishes the true Pyrenean, one of knowledge, valour, hardiness and intrepidity exemplified by Mr Belloc, whose like I could never aspire to equal. For 'like all things noble, the gourd has many subtleties besides. For instance, it is designed by Heaven to prevent any man abusing God's great gift of wine; for the goat's hair inside gives to the wine so appalling a taste that a man will only take of it exactly what is necessary for his needs'.

There was a surprising and immediate difference between this farthest corner of Spain and its near neighbour in France just across the Bidassoa. On the outskirts of the town there

45

were large tenement buildings, as in Hendaye; but whereas the latter were clean, neat and tidy, those in Irún gave the impression of imminent dereliction. Paint-starved back balconies were full of women and their hanging washing, children puddled below them in dust and junk, and people generally were so numerous that one felt one was looking at a disturbed ant-hill. This bewildering crush of people persisted into the centre of the town where, at the top of the hill in a square where stood a large, graceful but seedy renaissance house, I enquired at a bar for a small hotel. After I had made the mistake of ordering a French Kronenbourg beer—the only word around that I recognized—which cost the equivalent of four shillings, the barman directed me to a place in a street just opposite. Fonda Arrupe was a tall, four-storeyed building with a dismal entrance doorway beside a cavernous, dingy and apparently independent bar. My room, up a couple of flights of worn wooden stairs, gave on to a small airwell and was so dark that electric light was essential, and even then I have seen brighter coal cellars. But it was reasonably clean and the lady of the house was pleasant and business-like. After enquiring the hour of dinner and hearing it was at the distressing time of nine-thirty (quite early, actually, for Spain) I went out to look at the town.

Most of Irún lay on either side of a long, straight street that ran directly up the hill. It was thronged with people, who simply strolled about for want of anything else to do, the evening being warm and pleasant. It reminded me of Tunis in this respect. Street-thronging appears to be a characteristic of poor towns in warm countries; it is a popular and inexpensive pastime. The Plaza de España, for example, was a meeting place for nearly all the mothers and babies of the place, and there was quite a serious pram-jam.

Having worked out that one peseta was worth three halfpence, I bought a pocket Spanish-English dictionary (printed in Madrid) and felt better equipped to cope with this unfamiliar language. I returned to the bar in the square, where the barman spoke a little French, ordered a *pastis* and prepared to while away the evening. I was now able, from watching people, to detect the Basque physiognomy, the long, thin, dark face, the hooked nose; but among others I noticed a range of complexions, including fair and ginger, although darkness predominated.

Dinner time came at last and I climbed the gloomy staircase to the dining-room. The main course, preceded by soup and a dish of vegetables, was a fried flat fish, whose identity I did not try to establish; the wine was rougher and stronger than that to which I had become accustomed the other side of the border. I slept extremely well.

In the morning my ankle was still uncomfortable, so I decided on a short journey of only ten miles to give it a chance of recuperation. The weather was becoming clearer and the Fonda Arrupe's bill, much to my surprise, came to something like eighteen shillings altogether. After coffee in the bar in the square I set off gingerly down the road, past another square where rows of donkeys, the poor man's friend, were tethered. Coming round to the river bank again I approached Behobia and noticed in mid stream a small, long island, grown over with tall trees. The only sign of man upon its inconsiderable surface was a large monument of stone, with indiscernible writing on it. The curious thing about this island, called Isle of Pheasants, is that it has several times played a leading part in international politics. Since it constituted a kind of no-man's-land, the frontier being the river, it came to be used for a venue of sundry negotiations.

In 1525, after the Battle of Pavia, King Francis I of France was made prisoner by Emperor Charles V. The next year he was exchanged, rather like Miss Bun the Baker's daughter, for his two children, and the transaction took place on this little island. What the French king, or his children, thought or felt about it one can only imagine.

Ninety years later the Isle of Pheasants was chosen for a more felicitous occasion: France and Spain swapped princesses as brides for their respective kings, Elisabeth of France going to Philip III, and Anne of Austria (who, confusingly, was Spanish, like Chesterton's Don John of Austria, the 'last knight of Europe') to Louis XIII. Then, in 1659, it was used as a treaty-chamber (its other name is Île de la Conférence) when the Treaty of the Pyrenees was signed. This delineated the exact boundary, which had been subject to endless dispute and was until then extremely vague, between France and

Spain. The boundary was reviewed and again accepted in 1856, the treaty being agreed at the same venue, and the island itself was accorded a most peculiar status, becoming the property, alternately every year, of both countries. A Spanish viceroy ruled it from 1st February to 31st July, and a French viceroy (usually the commanding officer of their Bidassoa naval station) from 1st August to 31st January.

Biriatou

A short way upstream from the island, at the village of Behobia, was a bridge and frontier post, and beyond it the Bidassoa valley became increasingly delightful. The river shone between glowing green meadows, and hillsides rose to rocky heights stippled with spring verdure. On a steep hill on the French side was the lonely, small, truly Pyrenean village of Biriatou, about which Henry Myhill, in *The Spanish Pyrenees*, tells a lovely smuggling story. The Mayor and a dozen village elders were entertaining a customs officer, who with mounting consternation gathered that he was the only man among them who was not an habitual smuggler.

When the frontier between two countries is a river which is neither deep nor wide, and a disparity in prices between them means that profits can be made in one from selling goods bought in the other, then wet feet by night and police patrols by day are unavoidable. Walking along the road, alone, with a pack on my back, I was an obvious suspect, so I was stopped once by a Guarda Civil (who was very young and bored and really only wanted a chat) and twice by police cycling in pairs. There were several police stations and Guarda barracks along the way, and little whitewashed brick sentry-boxes every hundred yards or so.

The valley increased in beauty as it narrowed and the hills became mountains, and at a hamlet called Endarlaza the frontier left the river and sloped off up a mountain. I saw no more of the police or the Guarda Civil after that, except for routine village coppers. On the southern hillside above the village were two ancient round towers; down by the river there was a new hydro-electric plant, tastefully built of stone in the Basque style. One of the half-dozen houses that made up the place was a bar and I had a thirst, so I went in and had a drink.

Here I met an elderly man in forest green denims, who spoke a little French, and a young man with a broken arm who spoke a great deal of Spanish. The latter's arm was supported by an extraordinary metal frame which stuck out at right angles to himself; he had been like that, he said, for three months, ever since he fell off his motor-bike. He could sleep in no position but on his back, and badly there, and the straps of the frame cut into his neck. He went fishing for something to do, and seemed to be healthy and cheerful despite it all.

Endarlaza, where the frontier left the river, was also the border between the provinces of Guipúzcoa and Navarra, and this was marked by a large painted Navarrese coat of arms. The seven Basque Provinces, whose motto is *Zazpiak Bat* (Seven as One), are from west to east on the Spanish side: Vizcaya or Biscaya, capital Bilbao; Alava, capital Vitoria; Guipúzcoa, capital San Sebastian; and Navarra, capital Pamplona. On the French side, Labourd, from the sea-coast

to the Joyeuse valley; Basse-Navarre, which used to be part
of the Kingdom of Navarre; and Soule, in and around the
long and narrow Saison valley. The Spanish provinces, besides
outnumbering the French, are also of much greater area.
There are at present 200,000 French and 1,500,000 Spanish
Basques, not counting the tens of thousands dispersed all over
France and the Americas.

This totally charming Bidassoa valley was alive with colour:
not only the subtle shades of Arcadian green, but also the
yellows, blues, violets, and pink-and-whites of the spring
flowers, the yellow, orange and blue of the butterflies, and the
sudden flashing reds and yellows, blacks, greys and browns
of the quick little birds. There was also the shimmering shot-
silk of the river, and the silver springs of cool water from every
hillside.

I arrived in Vera, past a few small factories including one
making Izarra, the Basque liqueur, and probed around for
an inn. That was not easy, since the only labelled hotel was
severely closed; and although the people I asked could not
have been more courteous and helpful, my knowledge of
Spanish was so meagre that it was some time before I ran to
earth what appeared to be the only accommodation available
in the place. This was at Bar Txocoa, pronounced Choko, a
modern building in the old style run by a cheerful, hairy
young character whose wife spoke some French. The room
was small and quite filled by two beds, and the bathroom-
cum-lavatory across the passage had an atmosphere that
could not be endured for longer than five minutes at a time.
The bath appeared not to have been used that year, possibly
because there was no hot water.

Vera was a town in the middle of the widened Bidassoa
valley, and it was much intersected by tributary streams. Its
houses were almost identical with those in Espelette, with
none of Irún's air of squalor, and shop-names were undiluted
Basque. The church, at the top of the town, was tall and big
and built of stone in the sixteenth century, but having been
restored only four or five years ago it appeared nearly new.
Inside, it was very simple and bare, except for a huge,
elaborately gilded reredos and a big organ gallery and choir
stall.

Bar Txocoa, although new, was not a remarkably attractive place. The floor (of the bar itself, I mean) was filthy with a hundred cigarette-ends, and the walls, although recently distempered and tastefully decorated with painted murals, were succumbing to the advance of damp mottled stains. Into this idyllic nursery, while I was reading, writing and drinking away the long Spanish evening, came a little lad of perhaps eight years. Advancing confidently to the counter he slapped his money down and called for a drink. Solemnly the hairy young owner produced a glass and poured out some fizzy orange. The boy knocked it back in one go, grinned villainously at the assembled company, and left. A gap-toothed old man standing near caught my eye, laughed and gestured as if to say 'there's one that's learning the right way early.' The wisdom of this was demonstrated not five minutes later, when an unshaven, squat, weather-beaten old reprobate charged in, banged and shouted for service, and disposed of a full glass of wine in similar manner. The hairy one, drawing everyone's attention, including mine, to this, poured him another and they all shouted '*Porto! Porto!*' The old one put that away, still without drawing breath, and made to leave. '*Porto! Porto!*' Evidently his reputation would not allow departure until a third had been poured and engulfed. At last he was permitted to go, accompanied by loud cheers.

While I was searching, without success, in my new little dictionary for the meaning of the word *porto*, I noticed that while *posadera* was a landlady, *posaderas* were buttocks, and that *portarse* was to behave.

Dinner was at nine, in the little room beyond the bar. Several other diners kept me company, and although the menu turned out to be almost identical with that in Irún, the quality of cooking was better, the wine was enjoyable, and I rounded off the meal with an Izarra, fiery, sweet and pale amber.

I thought that the young owner had made some miscalculation when in the morning, after some coffee, I asked him for the bill. It was 110 pesetas, about thirteen and ninepence. Still, the bathroom did smell rather strongly.

I thought that while I was deep in Spanish Basque country I would sample some of their sausage, a type peculiar to them called *chorizo*. I would have bought a length of it, but the old lady at the general store was kindness itself: she sliced off a number of rounds, peeled off the skin, cut some bread in half and sold it to me as a ready-made sandwich. Belloc said that, with bread and the gourd-full of wine, it was ideal as the staple diet of Pyrenean explorers. 'You will soon', he added amiably, 'hate it, even if you do not, as is most likely, hate it from the bottom of your heart on the first day, but there is nothing else so compact and useful.'

It is a reddish compound of meat, garlic, tomato and fifty-seven other subtle ingredients, and I thought, when later I had the sandwich for lunch, that it was jolly good.

There were more factories on the other side of Vera, and a foundry, and a dirty, grey, gritty quarry. The weather that day possessed similar qualities, and a tendency to rain as well. For some of the way, continuing up the river valley, there ran a little aqueduct of swift-flowing water raised above the roadside. An oddity, I thought, in a place already running with water. I stopped at a large, square stone house which looked like a prison but was really an inn called 'Venta de Echalar', and tried the Spanish beer. It was similar in taste to the French, but not so fizzy. I was glad of that, because the first one went down with the despatch of the '*porto*' exponents at Bar Txocoa. My ankle was still sore, and it gave me a thirst.

It was at another place of refreshment of an entirely different character, some five miles farther up the valley towards Sumbilla, where I stopped for the same reason, that I learned a little of the Basque tongue. The bar-room, attached to a kind of transport café, was about two yards square, panelled with split logs, and entirely devoid of furniture, which grieved me because I wanted badly to sit down. However, leaning on the bar I got into conversation with the young lady of the house who spoke French.

'Are you', I asked, 'Basque, and do you speak your own language?'

'Yes, nearly everyone around here is Basque. In the family, we speak in Basque all the time.'

'I'm glad of that,' I said, 'because I have heard that often the young people do not learn it, and there is a danger that it will die out.'

'That may be the case in France, but in Spain we have Basque schools. There's one in Pamplona, another in San Sebastian. In France they learn only French at school, but here, even in our ordinary schools, we learn Basque. It is spoken a great deal by everyone.'

At the moment, providentially, two lorry drivers entered. The elder, a thickset swarthy man, said, '*Egunon.*' That, I knew, was Basque for 'Good day.'

I persuaded this young lady to provide for me a sample of the Basque tongue in writing, and this is what she wrote:

Aita guria zeruetan zaudena. Santificabedi zure
izena betor, gure gana zure izena eguin bedi zure
borondatea zerouan bezela lurrean ere.
Eman ezaguzu gaur gure eguneko oguia,
baka ezaguzu gure zorrak gu gueren
zorduenari barkatzen diegun bezela.

Agur.

It is the Lord's Prayer.

The antiquity of Euskara (the Basque word for it) is exceeded only by the difficulty in learning and understanding it. To demonstrate the first, a zealous bishop of the early nineteenth century proved that Adam and Eve spoke it. To illustrate the second, the Basques tell a story of how the Devil, trying to converse with a Basque, was so enraged at being unable to understand a single word that he jumped into the nearest river. It is considered perhaps the most ancient of the languages spoken in Europe, but scholars differ in opinion of its origin and roots, and most will not commit themselves. Except, of course, for the indefatigable George Borrow, who in *The Bible in Spain* commits himself as didactically as ever. 'Much', he says, severely, 'that is vague, erroneous, and hypothetical has been said and written concerning this tongue. The Basques assert that it was not only the original language of Spain, but also of the world, and that from it all other languages are derived; but the Basques are a very ignorant people, and know nothing of the philosophy of language.'

Borrow dismisses the theories that Euskara was derived from Phoenician or from Irish, and comes to a great pronouncement: 'To two great Asiatic languages all the dialects spoken at present in Europe may be traced.' These two tongues, he asserts, are distinct and widely different in structure: 'In what this difference consists I have neither time nor inclination to state; suffice it to say that the Celtic, Gothic and Sclavonian dialects in Europe belong to the Sanscrit family ... whilst to the Tibetan or Tartar family in Asia pertain the Mandchou and Mongolian, the Calmuc and the Turkish of the Caspian Sea, and in Europe the Hungarian and the Basque partially.'

While admitting that Euskara contains a number of words with Sanscrit roots, he comes down on the side of the Tartar origin. 'Whoever should have an opportunity of comparing the enunciation of the Basques and Tartars, would, from that alone, even if he understood them not, come to the conclusion that their respective languages were formed on the same principles.'

Pompous though Borrow might seem, his philological conclusions have been backed by modern scientific findings, as I shall demonstrate at a later point. The great puzzle is not so much where the Basques came from, as what happened to them when they settled on the Pyrenees.

There is evidence of Basque place-names over a much wider stretch of country than at present occupied by them: from the Garonne to the Pyrenees, in fact, and over into Spain. On the French side, this corresponds exactly with the territory held by the Nine Peoples, and one could easily, on philological grounds, make a case for the Nine Peoples all having been Basques, were it not for the decisive ethnological fact that the Basques are a distinct ethnic type and the rest of the territory is now occupied by people who are nothing like them at all. The case for the philologists is backed by the late Mr York Powell, once Regius Professor of History at Oxford, who, Belloc says, was 'capable of individual judgment in departments of living knowledge where his colleagues could but repeat words taught them from a book'. Gascony covers roughly this same area, from the Garonne to the Pyrenees, and the similarity between Gascon, the Latin Vascones, and Basque, is obvious. The dictum of this learned authority, Mr Powell, was that 'Gascon was Latin spoken by Basques'. Which seems quite plausible, but still does not explain the ethnic difference. The riddle, obscured by too many centuries past and complete lack of recorded history, may never be solved, but the game of guessing the solution is an intriguing one.

Nowadays, Euskara is spoken by an estimated 70,000 residents of the Basque Country, in eight different regional dialects. Naturally enough, it survives most strongly in the mountain valleys which are less influenced by outside pressures than the towns. I heard plenty of it spoken in the Baztan, for which I was now heading.

Shortly after leaving the bare little café and the pretty young Basque (incidentally the Spanish for Basque is *Vasco*), and the rain persisting, I was given a lift by a young couple in a fast sports car and taken to Santesteban, a village still farther up the Bidassoa valley. I went at once to the hotel that they recommended, but according to its proprietress it was at present non-operational. I started a tour of Santesteban, asking questions as in Vera, with the difference of dodging about in doorways because of the rain. Eventually I found 'Casa Maylin', a huge stone house where the reception was now in full swing for the wedding that we had seen emerging from the church in Sumbilla, on the way. I waited in the cold and primitive bar while they served interminable courses for the breakfast, the waitresses, who looked as if they all belonged to the Maylin family, rushing to and fro with tremendous sense of efficiency and the kitchen staff silent and sweating. The dancing had begun by the time I was shown to my room, and the music of an accordion thundered through the house. The noise gathered in volume, the music augmented by stamping, shouting, singing, and versions of the Irrintzina, the ancient Basque war-cry. This is an affair of the throat, a high-pitched yoyoyoyoy-yoy-yoy-YOY rising to an eerie, eldritch crescendo. Using the echoes in the mountains, it must have been unearthly, spine-chilling. Imagine Roland with Charlemagne's rearguard, caught and ambushed by the Basques at Roncesvalles, their doom heralded by a thousand of these ghastly cries.

The songs and the music were all strange to me, although the music had a distinctly Alpine flavour since all the verses seemed to end oompah-pah oompah-pah pah: Pah-Pah. I imagine that it was all indigenous stuff, and as there are more than two thousand different folk songs in the Basque tradition, they had plenty to choose from. In fact the song constitutes the popular literature of the Basques; love songs are the most popular because, it seems, the young bucks find it difficult to express their sentiments in ordinary speech. Since even the Devil found it difficult to express himself at all in the language, this is hardly surprising.

When I descended to the bar at about 6.30 I found it thronged with the wedding guests, who were pausing from their exertions on the dance floor to catch their breath and quench their thirsts. The latter objective was no problem, but the first must have been totally impossible because everyone found it necessary to communicate with his friends six inches away by shouting at the top of his voice. The noise, from two dozen conversations carried on at parade-ground volume, was unbelievable. Although the door was open to the pummelling rain outside and a cold breeze, all the revellers were shirt-sleeved and sweating (I was not); horseplay was boisterous but unfailingly good-natured, and everyone, young and old, men and women, bride and groom, was clearly determined to make the occasion memorable.

The accordionist struck up again; the drunkest of the sweating, fooling boys shouted '*Jota, jota!*' and grabbing the nearest girl charged back to the dance floor. At about half past eight one of the hotel people came to tell me that my dinner was now available, and ask what I would like. I went through to a room behind the dance floor, where they had cleared a space from the debris of the wedding-feast and where there were three other casual diners, youngish fellows who said they had driven from San Sebastián (a considerable distance) just to dine here.

It was easy to see why they had come. The meal was excellent: asparagus vinaigrette, and a steak grilled with strips of red peppers, a superb flavour. The accordionist, ensconced on a table, performed brilliantly (although his music, reverberating around the walls, nearly deafened us) and the dancers were still indefatigably at it. Those I had thought the noisiest and drunkest were those still on the floor executing the most complicated and rapid of (so my fellow-diners informed me) Navarrese dances. One of the waitresses, still in her black and white, who must have spent the entire day on her feet, joined in for a particularly fast and exhilarating *jota* in which the dancers, in single file, carried out a lightning series of steps, whirled around and circled the room. It made me wish I knew the steps and could join in.

At last, at ten o'clock, the accordionist, after a seven-hour stint on and off, packed up and went home, and the party ended.

Three or four of these same dancers, so gloriously drunk and yet capable of these high-speed dances, were in the bar at nine the next morning when I was having my coffee, still putting away an alcoholic measure or two. For such stone-headed resilience I had to admit the greatest respect.

The Bidassoa at Mugaire, four or five kilometres from Santesteban, was joined by the Baztan, which means for some curious reason 'rat's tail'. Villages in this valley were frequent, although it was V-shaped and narrow, and again the colours in the trees, the hundred shades of green, orange and russet, the flowering cherries and magnolias, everywhere gladdened the eye. The weather's perversity made it necessary often to seek shelter from monotonously frequent showers. In Arroyoz I dived into the village store, which sold everything that the human frame could require. In one dark corner a man was trying on a pair of new boots; at the counter two little girls waited while Señora weighed out their flour and counted up their bread and groceries; at the far end three elderly gentlemen stood talking over their glasses of red wine. These were joined by a remarkable old character in rubber boots, carrying a fishing rod; he had the indestructible, outdoor look of one who lives (probably in a hole in the river bank) slightly outside the law, and his ruddy, rustic joviality illumined the dark, busy little shop and had everyone laughing.

On the French side of the mountains the favourite candidates for road casualties appeared to be hedgehogs; here they were toads, huge ones, massacred by the score. Just out of Arroyoz, while I was stepping over the corpses, one of the younger patrons of the shop stopped his car and offered to take me to Elizondo, and as it had started to rain again I accepted. The hills on either side of the valley seemed no higher than the lower Black Mountains in Wales, which was strange since heights of three and four thousand feet were not far from them; the valley widened and we were in Elizondo, which was much larger than I expected. We passed a vast new hotel which the driver said was very expensive, and he dropped me in the main street near one which was not. This was the Hôtel Trinquete-Anchitonea, a typically Basque-featured building facing the bridge across the foaming brown Baztan. Attached to the hotel was the trinquet court (attached

Bridge at Elizondo

also to its name) where, this same afternoon, the semi-finals of the local paleta championship were to be held. I bought a ticket and went in.

Paleta is the indoor form of pelota and is played with a flat wooden bat (or palette, I suppose) and a hard black rubber ball. The court is deep and long; to watch, one sits in a high gallery along the side. The game is between two pairs of players; one of each pair plays forward, the other back. The ball is served against the end wall, and players of alternate sides must play it on the rebound. The ball can bounce off any of the forward three walls, the roof or the spectators, as long as it stays in play; points are scored when either side can no longer play it. There is a points system with games, sets and match, and the speed is terrific. To be expert requires electric reflexes, athletic agility and plenty of sheer beef, because the harder you hit the ball the faster it travels. The men I watched obviously had all these qualities, for the ball travelled like a bullet. The miraculous saves and returns had spectators, who included girls as well as men and boys, shouting, cheering, ooh-ing and aah-ing, and the whole match was the most tremendous fun.

The hotel had no restaurant of its own, so I went for dinner to one just opposite, on the riverside, and had a couple of delicious little trout, out of the Baztan so they said. It was Sunday night, and despite the incessant drizzle crowds of people were about.

In the morning there were two problems. One was my still very sore and uncomfortable ankle, the other was the dismally drenching rain. I waited until eleven o'clock for it to stop. It did not; but it had eased up a little, so I set forth, through the arcades, past the church of two towers (Elizondo means 'church in the valley': *eliz* is the same as the Welsh *egglws* and both come from the Greek ecclesia—Christianity brought its own vocabulary to all) and away from the town, still following the Baztan. In Arizcun I stopped to buy some more *chorizo* at a tiny shop-cum-bar presided over by a charming old sweat with no teeth, whose nose almost touched his lower lip. Then I pushed on to Errazu, the last village in Spain before the frontier.

The Customs in Errazu were in a vast stone house, in a lower room of which some policemen were sitting before a fire. I said I was going to France and they directed me vaguely upstairs, as if that was where France was. I climbed the massive stone staircase to the first floor and entered a pitch dark passage with not the slightest indication of which of the four or five doors was the right one. I picked the end one, for a start, and in the room was a little man fussing over a filing cabinet. I waved my passport at him and repeated that I wished to leave the country, and he produced a stamp, banged it on the passport and that was that. I wondered if there was a little man with a stamp behind each of the other doors.

I called at the last bar in the village, another of those magnificent all-purpose stores, to indulge for the last time in the amazing luxury of a glass of wine for three halfpence. I had learnt that to obtain this one needed only to approach the bar, slap a peseta on the counter, say '*Un vino tinto, por favor,*' and they would produce a little glass and half fill it with red wine.

It was still raining, with no promise of ever doing anything else, when I turned my back on Spain and took the road to the Col d'Ispeguy and France. The Aranea joined the Baztan at Errazu, and it was this narrow, steep, wildly lovely valley that I followed into the mountains. As I climbed the first of five miles of zigzags to the Col I could see, through the murk of the morose black clouds storming across the valley, the river winding steeply down between the green hills. Signs of human life were rare, but there were still occasional farmhouses, life in which, considering the distance even from little Errazu, must be what Henri de Becque called *pénible*. In all the time it took me to climb the zigzags to the Col through the driving rain, not more than three cars came by.

Up at the Col the two Spanish policemen viewed me with sympathy and apologized for their weather. It was no better on the French side of the border, but the view from the top made me feel I was really in the mountains at last.

Chapter Four

BASSE-NAVARRE

It was a weird prospect: the sombre outlines of the mountains, lurking under the heavy, ragged clouds, the steep wooded slopes, the black chasmal depths and the inevitable river buried somewhere at the very bottom.

After the eight kilometres up to the Col, there were another eight down to Saint-Etienne-de-Baigorry; the road, still devoid of any traffic save that of a lone, mad, wet Englishman, wound around each spur and re-entrant of the hills. Occasionally I would look back up to the Col and rejoice that, after the mild green hills of the Spanish side, here was something like the Pyrenees (although nothing at all like the High Pyrenees).

At last I came to Saint-Etienne, and crossed the Baigorry, which emerged from another ravine, not the one I had descended, and formed a wide, flat-bottomed valley. There were a four-towered château, a church and, incredibly, a railway station. Avoiding a large self-advertising hotel with a trinquet attachment (sure to be expensive) I found a quiet, comfortable and wholly excellent inn, 'Hôtel-Restaurant Juantoréna', where I began the process of drying off. Here was brought home to me as forcibly as with a school-marm's switch the lunatic folly of travelling with only one pair of trousers. The day had been, admittedly, by far the worst in all my walking career, but I felt keenly, as I sat in the bar sipping a *pastis* and pretending that they would dry on me (they did—eventually) that here was a flaw in my equipment in need of urgent attention, if ever I was to go travelling again.

The standard of all-round comfort, not to mention the hygiene, in the inn at Saint-Etienne-de-Baigorry was far higher than in those I had encountered on the Spanish side, and the bill, for a French inn, was surprisingly low, only just over a pound sterling all told. But then, like Guiche, Saint-Etienne is not exactly on anyone's normal touring itinerary.

Which is hard luck on the normal tourist, but a wondrous good thing for a broken-down traveller on foot.

The truth about those platforms in the trees of the Forest of Saint-Pée came to me in Saint-Etienne. The latter is noted for pigeon-hunting: in the autumn they stretch nets across the cols, like that of Ispeguy, and the migrating pigeons fly into them. The platforms in the trees are for the marksmen, who bang off their guns as the pigeons fly past. Clearly a forest would be an attraction to the pigeons, even one as far from the mountains as that of Saint-Pée, so the platforms were built for *la chasse*.

Trout fishing is also popular in Saint-Etienne, from the Baigorry, a typically Pyrenean stream which rattles along a wide, shallow bed.

Feeling in a poor state after yesterday's march I hobbled very sedately out of Saint-Etienne, over the bridge just downstream from an ivy-grown, hump-backed bridge dating from 1661 and nowadays used by nothing heavier than dogs or sheep. The rain, still with me, stopped for a while and I was just engaged in climbing the first real hill of the day when a man offered me a lift to Saint-Jean Pied-de-Port, which was that day's destination.

A keen-featured fellow of about my own age, the driver soon demonstrated that he was as interested in people and their languages and origins as I was, and it was he who provided the scientific guide to the Basques' origin.

'East of a line from Finland to, say, Turkey,' he explained, 'over 17% of the population are of the blood-group B. West of the line less than 17% are of this group—except for the Basques, who are again over 17% group B. That proves that they are ethnically similar to, say, the Tartars.'

I was not too sure that it proved anything of the sort, because the whole population of Europe drifted over from Asia originally. I have read since that the learned doctors Eyquem and Saint-Paul of the Pasteur Institute in Paris, finding that the Basques are in fact 60% O group and 27–35% Rhesus negative (whatever that means: my ignorance is absolute), have concluded that the Basques 'represent the pure descendants of the people who occupied Europe in Paleolithic times and, throughout the continent, were crossed with Asian invaders'. To the Basques' ancestors these pre-historians attribute the Franco-Cantabrian civilization, which at the end of the Paleolithic Age stretched from Santander to the Dordogne.

Now this sounds like sense to me: it explains the occurrence of Basque place-names north and south of the Pyrenees in territory never known to have been occupied by Basques, and it explains why the pure, uncrossed survivors, still existing in their corner of Europe, speak a language nothing like any other. If one presumes that they, before they occupied Europe, came from Asia like every other race that has ever populated Europe (even Aeneas of Rome was a Trojan from Asia Minor), then they might well still share some characteristics of biology, as suggested by my friend in the car, and of language, as insisted by George Borrow, with the Tartars.

What no one has yet been able to explain is why a race of less than two million people should have remained throughout all recorded history pure and distinct, their language intact, thousands of years after the rest of their tribe became Gauls and Iberians.

The driver, a most interesting man who spoke a little English and said he knew a lot of German (of which I am quite ignorant), was another protagonist for United Europe. He had travelled, was sophisticated and civilized, and it seemed to him the obvious and inevitable future for the Continent, providing, he said, that more of us took the trouble to learn properly at least one language besides our own.

He put me down in the square at Saint-Jean Pied-de-Port, and when he had gone I looked around for an inn. There were plenty from which to choose, and after drawing a couple of blanks and avoiding the grandest, I found a room in the Hôtel Etchandy, at the top end of the main road from the square. The room was actually in a house next door to the hotel, and two floors up as usual, but it was perfectly good and would do very well for the two nights I proposed to stay in the town.

In the afternoon, after changing back my Spanish money into French and collecting letters from home (at last) from the post office, I went to a cobbler in Rue d'Espagne, a cobbled (*sic*) street leading steeply up from the bridge by the church tower. I leaned over his window-sill and told him I had a slight problem.

'My shoes', I said, 'are in urgent need of repair. The heels are quite destroyed. But I have only the one pair; could you mend them while I wait?'

'Well, I have other work . . . but yes, I will do it. Come in and sit down.'

Sitting in his littered workshop, I watched, fascinated, the process of removing the ruins of the old heels, of tracing the outline, of building up the new heels, with layers of stout leather, of driving in the brads, of smoothing and paring and polishing. 'Shall I', he asked, 'put steel tips on them? And on the toes?'

He made an excellent job of them; well pleased, I paid him his price, which was not high, and walked back to my hotel feeling an inch or two taller.

This little fortified town of Saint-Jean Pied-de-Port has a long and varied history, principally because it is situated on one of the oldest routes through the Pyrenees, that of Ronces-valles. This, naturally enough, the Romans used, and their depot was at Saint-Jean-le-Vieux, a mile or two to the east. Roncesvalles is about eighteen miles to the south, and its name is universally renowned, largely because of an eleventh-century poem, the *Chanson de Roland*. This embroidered romantically a dark and tragic legend, and became an instru-ment for stirring up the Christian world for further effort against the Saracens who had colonized Spain for some four hundred years. In fact the villains of the legend were not the Moslem Moors, but the allegedly Christian Basques.

In the year A.D. 777 the Emperor Charlemagne, ruler of the Franks, was requested by one Sulaiman ben Alarabi, governor of Barcelona, to help him in a conspiracy against the Caliph, Abd-ar-Rahman. Charlemagne, seeing an opportunity both to strengthen guard on the southern frontier of his empire and to give some assistance to the suppressed Christians of Spain, formed an army and in the spring of 778 marched south. Passing through various of the Pyrenean routes, he entered Navarre and arrived in Pamplona. Life was not easy even in Navarre; its inhabitants, the Basques, although supposedly Christian, were in the habit of fighting Franks, Moors and

Asturians (from the small remaining Christian Spanish kingdom) indiscriminately.

In Pamplona he learnt that his ally Sulaiman had taken
Saragossa, so he marched there, only to find that it was held
by another, hostile Saracen chief. He does not appear to have
done anything about this, but instead he marched farther
south and ravaged Huesca, Barcelona and Gerona, all fortress
towns and a danger to the routes through the mountains to
his own domains. He then returned to Pamplona, and as it
constituted too isolated an outpost, beyond the mountains, to
hold against the Moors and was presumably too convenient
a stronghold to leave for them to occupy, he somewhat un-
diplomatically burnt it to the ground.

This infuriated the Navarrese Basques, who, not from any
great nationalistic feeling but more in the role of brigands,
cast their eyes upon the riches collected by the Emperor's
army and now proceeding slowly north in his baggage train,
and vowed vengeance. In view of the fact that his army had to
pass through the mountains and that he had enraged the
Basques whose territory they were, it would appear unwise,
to say the least, for the Emperor to march on ahead with his
army and leave the baggage train in charge of a small rearguard; but that is what he did.

'Here', writes Hilaire Belloc, 'was a prodigious cleft running
dead north, thousands of feet sunk sheer into the earth, and
slowly widening its sides to where, far away at the opening of
it in the misty distance, in the V-shape mouth of the hills,
like a calm sea in misty weather, lay the Gascon plains.' The
rearguard and the cumbrous waggons, all loaded with the
riches filched from looted towns and palaces, toiled laboriously
up the narrow path, in zigzags like that of the Col d'Ispeguy.
Not a sign of life could be seen, and Roland of the Breton
Marches, and Eggihard the Seneschal, and Anselm the Count
Palatine, commanders of the column, saw no reason for des-
patching patrols, or outposts, or flanking parties: 'In that
profound ravine there was no noise at all except the running
of the torrent in the forest below. The walls were very steep,
so steep, that in places the beech-trees had lost their hold
and had fallen down the precipitous earth; and perilously
along the front of that slope went the road.'

As evening came and the defile, deserted by the sun, darkened, the shadows on the steep hillsides seemed to move, a chill crept into the marching men, a dreadful apprehensive fear of something unimaginably frightful that was about to happen to them. . . .

Darkness had not quite come when, like half-expected thunder, a huge boulder crashed down the mountainside, bounding destructively upon them, smashing its way to the ravine's floor. Suddenly the air was filled with scores of bloodcurdling, unearthly cries that froze their minds and made them babble prayers for mercy. Then the human avalanche fell on them. The knights, the noblest and bravest of all, forced their way through the crush of waggon and team and struggling men, but it was too late for valour. Before midnight there was not one of the Emperor's rearguard left alive.

Saint-Jean Pied-de-Port is, and always has been, the capital of Basse-Navarre. I went in the morning to inspect it (I will pass over the evening's dinner—it gave me indigestion), starting down the hill to the square, on the northern side of which stood a fine stone Renaissance house called Maison de Mansard which is now the Mairie. I made my way, through an arch in the walls and through another arch immediately under the church tower, to the river. There was a sign which said 'Roman Bridge, 500 metres', so I strolled (or, rather, limped: you cannot properly stroll with a bad ankle) along the beautifully wooded riverside until I found it. It looked no older than any other single-arched, hump-backed, narrow little bridge, and in fact I suspect that although its foundations and base stones may be as the Romans left them, a good deal of it has been replaced, knocked down and built up again since.

I returned along Nive-side, greeting on the way a cheerful young lad off to his sheep, and entered the church. This, Notre-Dame du Pont, although the arch-pierced tower was built in the eleventh century, is mainly of the eighteenth. It was dark, simple for a Catholic church; the Stations of the Cross on the walls were written in Basque, and there was a large wooden gallery at one end. There were also hymn-books in the Basque tongue.

Leading up from the church was a very steep street lined on both sides by some of the oldest and finest houses in the town,

Saint-Jean Pied-de-Port

of which the oldest was some four hundred and the newest one hundred years of age. Half way up the street, on the left, was a building older than any, a long, narrow, barn-like structure of stone, taller at the far end because of the fall of the hillside. This was the Bishops' Prison. The door was open, so I entered. In a small dark vestibule, with a wooden staircase leading up to a closed door, there were some simple curios including a case full of swords and spears, a stuffed and mounted boar's head of ferocious aspect, and a huge coat-of-arms of Navarre made out of real chains. The same design, that of a cross and saltire of chain, functions for both Spanish and French Navarre: it commemorates an ancient victory of Christians over Saracens, at Las Navas de Tolosa in 1212. The Navarrese played an important part by breaking the ranks of the personal bodyguard of the Sultan Miramolin, who were chained together for additional strength. The chains, and a large emerald with which the Sultan had rashly decorated the top of his tent, they bagged as trophies. The fate of the emerald does not appear to be recorded. Perhaps the feeling of righteousness at fighting for instead of against the Christian armies compelled the Navarrese Basques to give it to charity—perhaps they had second thoughts and kept it for themselves.

While I was contemplating these objects in the vestibule, the concierge, suddenly coming in from the street and finding me there unexpectedly, started, cried 'Oh, la la,' then composed herself sufficiently to charge me the customary entrance fee of one franc, give me a ticket, open the door and switch on the taped commentary guide. It was very dark, despite sundry low-powered electric lights. I clambered down a greasy flight of worn stone steps to the nethermost dungeon, lit only by a tiny window high up in the wall. Old chains hung from the walls, the floor was of damp beaten earth, and there was a slope at one end where the prisoners could get what rest it afforded. The voice of the tape-recorder, enunciating slowly and carefully and relayed to such cavernous depths by amplifiers, was meanwhile telling me that the prison, although called the Bishops' Prison, was not a prison *for* bishops but *of* bishops, and that it was actually used for the incarceration of 'false pilgrims'.

The bones of Saint James having been discovered in the

ninth century, in obedience to the directions of a miraculous
star over a remote village called Compostela on the Biscayan
coast, the resulting shrine became a source of inspiration to
the Christian cause of driving out the alien, infidel Saracen
from Spain. It was also for many years a magnet for Christian
pilgrims from all over Europe, and in due course their routes
were organized in a way that would be considered pretty
efficient even by modern standards. The main routes, by
Hendaye, the Col d'Ispeguy and Roncesvalles, were scarcely
five miles without a chapel, an oratory or church for the
spiritual needs of the pilgrims, who were equally well and
more practically provided with hostels and lodging houses.
Here the pilgrims might obtain rest, shelter, food and a change
of clothes, since many came long distances and wore away
their shoes and clothes to rags. In fact the pilgrim routes to
Compostela were superintended by an international tourist
organization with a chain of hotels and its own health service,
highway guards and printed guide—all completely free of
monetary charge.

The prison which I was inspecting, with that disembodied
voice booming away sepulchrally at me in all corners, was part
of the service. Human nature being for ever perverse, there
were those who would take advantage of the honest piety of
genuine pilgrims, and pose as their fellows and travelling com-
panions. Having gained their confidence with, no doubt,
apparently well-meaning acts of charity and quiet mention of
well-established prosperity, these mediaeval con-men would
choose a moment to rob, strip and sometimes murder them.
The highway guards, having arrested the villains, would con-
sign them to this ghastly dungeon, and serve them right.

In one of the upstairs cells—a little airier and less obviously
lethal—was a collection of photographs of modern pilgrims
and of the Abbey at Roncesvalles, which was part of the
organization and throve because of it. I was so engrossed that
time went by, the ghostly voice started its recital all over
again, and the concierge, perhaps wondering if I had succumbed to the atmosphere of the place by maniacally locking
myself in one of the cells, came to enquire if I had finished my
tour.

Out in the daylight again—I should like to say sunlight

but it was again cloudy—I continued to climb the precipitous little street until, at the top, I came to the Citadel. This reminded me strongly of the toy forts we used to have as children, with ramps winding up in front, and drawbridges and gatehouses, and walls and towers and turrets and battlements. Climbing up the winding ramp, under the drawbridge, up to the battlements, feeling like one of those little red-coated leaden soldiers with a perpetually surprised expression and his rifle barrel inevitably broken off short, I reached a rampart where I could look back to the château buildings, across the drawbridge, and before me to the whole of Saint-Jean, its walls, the plain, and the Nive where it squeezed itself between the mountains.

The old, outer walls of the town were erected in the fifteenth century, the second, inner ring of walls and the castle itself according to Vauban's plans in the seventeenth. There had been, of course, a succession of castles on the site from very earliest times, from Roman imperial times onwards, so obvious was the site's strategic value. This was still true at the time of the Peninsular Campaign when, in 1813, the Duke of Wellington tentatively invaded France. Since his Pyrenean movements covered much of the ground I had just walked through, a broad outline of them might here be of some interest.

On 21st June 1813 the French army in Spain was overwhelmingly defeated at Vitoria, capital of the Basque province Alava, by Wellington's combined force of British, Portuguese and Spanish troops. So great was the disorder in which they retired that they left behind all their artillery and baggage (including all their loot). They fled by the one narrow road available to Roncesvalles and France, and the reign of 'King' Joseph Bonaparte, the Emperor's brother, came to an end. While Wellington arranged his army to cover the frontier, Marshal Soult, despatched by Napoleon, arrived to reorganize the French troops, a task at which he excelled. Wellington invested San Sebastián and Pamplona, which were still held by the enemy, and disposed his troops along the Bidassoa and the Baztan, to check the passes from Maya (north of Elizondo; I turned off right, eastwards, to Col d'Ispeguy) to Roncesvalles.

On 25th July Soult began his first attempt to relieve Pamplona; his troops advanced to the passes of Maya and Roncesvalles, but without, it seems, very great determination, for at Maya they were repulsed by the British under Sir Rowland Hill, and at Roncesvalles Byng's brigade managed to keep them in check. Wellington, trying from his head-quarters in Lesaca, five miles from Vera, to deduce Soult's intentions, rode to the Baztan, arriving at 4.00 a.m., to find that although Hill had retired down the valley to cover Elizondo the French had not followed him up. Wellington then rode to Almandoz, on the road to Pamplona, where he received a cheerless despatch from Cole, commander of the force holding Roncesvalles, to the effect that, although the pass was being held quite capably, he was beating a retreat. Unused to high command, he had succumbed to the strain of responsibility and wanted to shift it on to the shoulders of Picton, at Pamplona. In point of fact the French were in no state to take much advantage of this, having lost their way in the mountains.

Wellington joined Picton and Cole at Sorauren, a village some six miles from Pamplona, and there on the 28th received the attack of Soult's forces which had come down from the mountains and joined up. They were repulsed with consider-able loss, and fled once more to the mountains, where they were chased down the Bidassoa through Santesteban and Sumbilla and over the Pass of Echalar back into France.

A month later, on 31st August, Soult tried to relieve San Sebastián. An army of 45,000 men crossed the Bidassoa, under cover of a thick mist, between Vera and Irún. The Spanish garrison of the hill of San Marcial, opposite Biriatou, threw them back and chased them across the river. On the same day Wellington's troops took San Sebastián, and regrettably disgraced themselves by an orgy of looting, drinking and raping.

Wellington was now in full command of the frontier and was being requested to invade France. He hesitated to do so because he was not in sufficient strength without the Spanish troops. These were neither paid nor fed by the Spanish Government, and would therefore have to exist by plundering the countryside, which Wellington was anxious to avoid in the interests of good relations with the local populace. Eventually he compromised by taking over 4,000 of them on his own payroll, and on 7th October crossed the Bidassoa without undue trouble at a point below the Isle of Pheasants, where some Basque shrimpers showed him a ford across the mud-flats which was known to them only. His troops advanced some three miles farther up the Bidassoa and commanded the heights overlooking the western plains. Soult had organized his defences in three lines, the first of which Wellington's men now occupied, that of the heights above the Bidassoa. The second followed the Nivelle from Saint-Jean-de-Luz to Ascain, the Mondarrain mountain mass behind Espelette, and thence to Saint-Jean Pied-de-Port. The third followed the course of the Nive to the fortified city of Bayonne, wherein lay a considerable arsenal.

On 31st October Pamplona at last succumbed to the siege, and a week later, on 9th November, Wellington attacked Soult's forces between Sare and the Nivelle at Saint-Pée, and once more routed them. Soult abandoned the defences of Saint-Jean-de-Luz and retreated to his positions along the Nive from Cambo to Bayonne. These Wellington attacked on 9th December, crossing the Nive quite easily between Cambo and Ustaritz, and advanced on the south-eastern defences of Bayonne. The main part of his army was still distributed between this advanced position and the sea, and it was here that Soult, in the celebrated Sortie from Bayonne, tried to break out on 12th December. Although he made some progress his men were eventually checked and repulsed, and on the 13th he tried the other way, throwing six divisions against Hill's force in the hills above Saint-Pierre d'Irube, south-east of Bayonne. Here he nearly succeeded: Hill's reinforcements had not arrived, the Nive was in spate, a temporary bridge had been swept away, and two of his colonels let him down badly, one of them ordering his battalion to retreat and the other running away personally. Rowland Hill was not given overmuch to fulmination, but this was too much even for him. When a report of what he said to one of the errant colonels came to Wellington, he observed, 'If Hill is beginning to swear we had better get out of the way.'

At all events, the remainder of Hill's men were of sterner

stuff, and held their ground. Soult gained little and lost a great number of men, including several German battalions which deserted to the other side.

During the two-month stagnation of winter, when road conditions made movements impossible, Soult's army was depleted to make good the casualties suffered by Napoleon at his defeat at Leipzig. On 14th February, leaving a force to invest Bayonne, Wellington marched eastward, sweeping the French before him. Soult made a stand with six divisions at Orthez on the 27th, but was beaten again. Wellington marched on, and by 10th April was at the gates of Toulouse, where Soult was embattled with his whole army of 42,000 men. The battle, which was one of the bloodiest of the whole campaign, and resulted in Soult's retreat and abandonment of the city, was not even necessary: Napoleon had abdicated on the 8th, but the news did not reach the south-east until the 12th.

Wellington was praised by all sides and hailed as the Liberator of Europe. His had been one of the most persistently successful campaigns in all British military history.

The castle of Saint-Jean Pied-de-Port, although used throughout by Soult as a garrison and depot, was never attacked; by the time Wellington's allied armies reached it the garrison had long been withdrawn. The buildings, which have been recently repaired, are now used as a holiday centre for children. I could see them at the windows, and hear their shouts and laughter carried clearly on the still air. So was the church bell, tolling mournfully for a funeral procession which I could see winding its serpentine way very slowly along the road from Ispoure.

When I came down from the castle I fancied a cup of coffee and a *gâteau Basque* (a proper one, this time) by way of elevenses. It just so happened that I had picked the day when almost all the small shops, bars and cafés had staged a one-day strike. This, which they called a policy of *rideaux baisses* (lowered curtains), was a protest against iniquitous taxation which they claimed was forcing them to raise their prices out of proportion to values. Eventually I found a small shop in Rue d'Espagne that had stayed open, and took my cake to the path by the Nive to eat. It was much spicier and tastier than those apologies from Saint-Jean-de-Luz.

Rain started to fall again, and so did the temperature; I retired to my hotel. In the evening, while waiting for my meal (and because of the strike I was the only person allowed to have one), I overheard M. Etchandy, a long, thin, grey man with a big Basque nose, observe mournfully when he came in from his customary walk down town: 'The place is completely dead. Not a café open, not a restaurant, not a bistro, nothing.' No one, not even the most ardent *rideaux baisses* protester, could put up with that sort of thing for longer than a day. Dinner, of thick soup, and lamb, bacon and onions, was better than the previous night's, but the pork I would have preferred was not available: '*C'est la grève, Monsieur!*'

I had left some clothes with a very efficient and business-like washerwoman the day I arrived in town, and I had to wait until noon of the next but one to collect them. I called at the post office to post some letters and see if there were any more for me, and encountered a ferocious old battleaxe, grim as an ogre, who made me wait while she carried on writing for quite some minutes, without a word. Eventually she looked up, scowled at me and said '*Pour quoi?*' Of course there were no letters, her attitude seemed to imply: how dare I interrupt her important work with such trifling requests?

I left the town at half past twelve, although it was again raining. The road, after Ispoure, was dead straight for a couple of miles, past a tiny church called La Magdelaine, which looks like a sanctified barn, a rectangle of russet stone with a tower and spire as tall as the building is long. It is a delightful little church, a miniature with painted ceiling, wooden gallery and vastly over-elaborate altarpiece in the style of the Basques, all within about sixty feet by twenty. In the churchyard, moreover, are some typically angular and decorated tombstones, also in the local fashion: a place not to be missed. I missed it that time, because I had been there before, and it was raining.

On the outside edge of Saint-Jean-le-Vieux was the grassy outline of what, to my untrained eye, looked like a primitive earthwork: a kind of raised platform with steep edges. If it was, then this was the only remaining visible evidence that the village was the Roman fort and depot of Nine Peoples times.

After the village the road took me into hillier country, with
the hint of mountains behind the clouds. I stopped for a while
in La Carre, a pretty village squatting on a sloping hill below
a small château, spired and turreted and mostly shuttered,
but still inhabited. There are not many châteaux in the Basque
Country, because the Basques have never evolved, in their
democratic society, an aristocracy to build them.

In the hamlet of Mongelos, a little farther on, I looked for
a house where I had been once before.

One autumn day, some four or five years earlier, I left
Saint-Jean Pied-de-Port in the afternoon. By four o'clock I
felt a thirst coming on, and in Mongelos looked out for a café.
The village was not large, and I was beginning to fear that it
did not rate one when I spotted, outside the huge arched doorway of one of its old houses, the enamelled licence-plate
exhibited by all bistros. Even then I hesitated, because it
looked like any private house; but just then an old woman
came out and I asked her about it. She smiled, greeted me
warmly and showed me into what appeared to be her kitchen.

A large, dimly lit room, one wall seemed to be nearly all
fireplace: the shining brass battalion of ornaments on the
mantelpiece glimmered fitfully in the light of a flickering log
fire, before which sprawled three dogs. In one of the fireside
chairs sat a young woman, in the other a chicken. Near the
window was a large table round which sat five men, all wearing their berets, all drinking red wine and all talking very
loudly at once. As I entered, there was none of the instant-
oyster stoppage of conversation such as one finds in some
places: they managed to welcome me, sit me down and pour
me a drink without abating their talk in the least. Although
until then they had been talking in Euskara, for my benefit
they spoke in French, asking me questions out of friendly
interest, until someone got the cards out and they started
playing Muss, which is a form of poker using Spanish cards,
very popular among the Basques on both sides of the Pyrenees.
They kept me talking with them, and insisted on refilling my
glass; when I protested they said, 'No, Monsieur, please drink
with us: we are Basques, it is our custom.'

When I rose to leave, the young woman seemed glad only
to charge for my first glass of wine, and everyone was anxious

to shake hands and contribute their good wishes. Their good humour, their kindliness ('The chicken, Monsieur, was small and sick and the others bullied it, so we took it in and nursed it: now it is a household pet') and the warm, human atmosphere of the room stayed with me for a long time as a memory.

I knew it would not be the same, if I went back there; things never are. But I could not even go back there, because it was no longer a bistro: the house was empty, in the process of being renovated, and within the great arched doorway was a nasty, vulgar, new front door.

There were two new hotels in Mongelos that were not there before, and I stopped at neither of them.

A few miles farther on, with the weather beginning to improve and the luxuriant countryside brightening in the splashes of sunlight, a police van pulled up near me and its occupants asked me the usual questions and examined my passport. They offered to take me to Larceveau, which I thought was rather decent of them, but they really wanted to establish for sure that I was who and what I said I was, which they achieved by a radio consultation, in the Gendarmerie, with some mysterious authority which appeared to be omniscient enough to verify the details they read out to it (with hilariously wrong pronunciation); after quite a long wait they returned my passport and let me go. Outside, I asked the more human of the two policeman why they had gone to all this trouble. 'Just a routine check. You are staying here in Larceveau tonight? There is the hotel, over the road.'

The hotel, a modern attachment to an old house, was so new it was not yet finished, and I wondered if they would accommodate me. They would, they said, if I did not mind bare passages and paintless doors, and in fact they had one room with a bed ready made up. It had a balcony and a lovely view of the woods, fields and hills, and obviously, when it is finished (the people, a young couple, are doing it themselves), it will be a fine place.

Chapter Five

SOULE

Larceveau was a small village, not much more than the two hotels—the second with a trinquet court attached to it—and a few houses, a fronton and a church. Cibits, the next village along the road into the hills, was smaller still, and thereafter for several miles there were no villages at all. There were several houses, mostly of stone, slate-roofed, but all bore over the front-door lintel a large inscribed slab telling who built the house and when, and often embellished with a typically Basque symbol, the Lauburu. This word means 'four heads', which describes the device: a kind of female swastika, with curves instead of hard angles. It is a variety of the ancient sunwheel symbol, a survivor from very early, pre-Christian times; the Basques are peculiarly attached to it and add it to exterior and interior decoration of their houses and many other designs, such as ceramics and brassware.

The weather was showing signs of improvement that morning, and by the time I was half way to Saint-Just-Ibarre the sun was turning the heavenly, quiet, serene valley into an idyllic paradise. There were farms, mostly of a pastoral nature, green everywhere in all its shining spring colours, ox-teams of heavy yellow beasts carting and ploughing, and little splashing silvery streams. One of these I discovered was the Bidouze, which I had last encountered at its farthest end, the slow muddy river beside which I had walked from Bidache to Guiche.

At Saint-Just I indulged my predilection for sitting in the sunshine outside a café and sipping red wine. I had not been able to do so very often on this journey because there had not until then been a surplus of sunshine. The café, an ancient house, stood beside the steeply mounting road, and its terrace was lightly shaded by an arcade of blooming, bee-mumbling wistaria. One could sit, wave benignly at passers-by and

Larceveau

admire the Arcadian landscape at the foot of the sharply
rising wooded hills.

Refreshed and in good humour I started the climb up to
the Col d'Osquich, where the hills grew into small mountains
and barred the way between Basse-Navarre and Soule,
negotiable by this one pass. The road climbed gradually,
without insisting on undue exertions, and compared with Col

d'Ispeguy it was easy, and much more pleasant because the weather was now ideal. Traffic was infrequent and I could listen at leisure to the sheep-bells and cuckoo-calls, and notice the bright little blue and yellow and white hill-flowers, and the scurrying lizards, and the chapel of Saint-Antoine on the crest of the opposite hill, across the ravine that fell away from the col.

At the top there was a hotel where I was refreshed with a glass of beer, sitting in the kitchen while the owner and his wife worked quietly, competently and harmoniously at various culinary tasks. There was also the superb view of the other side of the col, where the mountains formed a wide basin of wonderfully peaceful green farm-land, another cul-de-sac valley with scattered white farmsteads under the vague collective name of Pagolle. I chose a wayside tree-trunk on which to sit and eat my lunch, overlooking this view; fifty yards back a new hotel, called Bista Eder (which means 'beautiful view') shared it. Large hawk-like birds, which I took to be eagles, wheeled and floated high over the valley. The sun shone, the cow-bells tinkled, peace and contentment came drifting down from the green hill tops on the soft breeze.

Where the road crept around the top of the hill and emerged on the other side, another splendid panorama opened before me. It was the beautiful valley of the Saison, richly coloured with all the shades of green created by nature, fringed with wooded hills and backed by higher hills and the shadowy shapes of the great snowy peaks behind them. I was in Soule, the smallest of all the Basque provinces and the last, going eastward, of those on the French side of the mountains.

There were not many users of the road, and much of my walk down from the hills was in blissful, peaceful solitude. A young couple, sitting on the heathery bank near their car, offered me a lift, but after stopping for a chat with them I declined because the sun was so unusually warm and the way to Mauléon was all downhill. A stout farm worker, in beret and blue overalls, rode up the road on his motor-cycle and shouted and waved cheerfully at me. These apart, I met few fellow-travellers until I came down into the village of Musculdy. Here I looked for an aged, grey stone house in which I had stopped for a drink on my previous expedition. It had vanished; its site was occupied by a large, brand new white-washed Hôtel de Chistera. Its frontal view, across the lane to the little church, the fronton and the rather untidy greensward, had not changed in the least. I climbed the steps to the new hotel and entered the long, clean, characterless bar-room.

But the manager, a solidly built man of about forty with black hair and moustache, could not have been more affable. I asked him about the old stone house where I had sat in a cool room after a similar descent from the Col d'Osquich and had enquired of the ginger-haired young woman who served me the age of the house: 'I don't know, Monsieur,' she had said, 'but it is certainly very old.'

'Yes,' said the manager of Hôtel de Chistera, 'it was very old, and it was in such a bad state that it was not worth repairing, so when my *Patron*, who is an Englishman, a very decent man, bought it he had it pulled down and this new one built.'

'Are you a local man, a Basque?'

'No, my wife and I worked for this same Englishman in Paris. When he built this hotel he asked us if we would like to manage it, and we were only too glad to escape from the city. It is very lovely here, we like it. Tell me, do you follow Rugby? What do you think of Wales this year?'

We discussed the sport, which is more popular in the South-West than anywhere else in France, and after a while and a couple more glasses of wine moved on to politics. What, he asked me, did the English think of de Gaulle nowadays? Would they be glad, considering that he refused to allow Britain to join the Common Market, if he resigned as President?

'Some', I suggested, 'might, but many would prefer France to be stable rather than anarchic. The events of May last year were worrying; after all, if de Gaulle were to go, who would be as strong a president as Monsieur Cohn-Bendit?'

The manager of Hôtel de Chistera appeared to find this possibility hilariously funny.

It was a long way to Mauléon, and by the time I had covered half of it the kilometres seemed inexplicably long, my ankle was becoming more painful and I wished I had stayed in Musculdy. I stopped at another of my old haunts, a wayside bar with a dance-floor at Garindein called 'Le Coucou des Bois', but it was smaller than I had remembered and had no accommodation for travellers. 'In any case,' they said, 'the noise of the dances is so immense that no one would be able to sleep.'

I hobbled on and eventually reached the town of Mauléon, where I settled for the first hotel I came to. This is nearly always a mistake for various reasons—too expensive or too shabby or too bad—but I was too tired to look any farther so took a chance.

This one, Hostellerie du Château, was quite good, but since ex-President René Coty had once been entertained there it was disposed to charge a little more than was really warranted. But I was grateful enough for a bed on which to subside for an hour or so, and a good dinner with the usual comforting half-litre of red wine while successive politicians, on the television, exhorted the assembled company to vote *oui* or *non* on 27th April. A young man with his family at the next table was constrained to vote *oui* to buying one of two irresistible Alsatian pups presented at his table: he grinned sheepishly at me as if to say, 'Yes, I know I'm probably a fool to do it, but the kids will love him and he is rather adorable, don't you think?'

In the morning I discovered that the inflamed tendon in my left ankle had been joined, probably in sympathy, by the calf muscles in my right leg. It occurred to me as I hobbled, perspiring, down the stairs, that for a man on a walking tour I presented a ludicrous spectacle. Leaving my gear in the hotel I meandered slowly around town. It was sunny, but not so warm as it had been the day before.

Mauléon is built on both banks of the Saison (also called Gave de Mauléon) and it has a fourteenth-century castle on a hill, a splendid renaissance mansion called Hôtel d'Andurain, a large, tree-lined square incorporating the Municipal Fronton, and several factories for the production of shoes and sandals. The Basque type of sandal is called *espadrille* and is rope-soled. Properly it should be tied with a complicated system of tapes round the leg, but these are effete times and it is now worn with just blue canvas over toes and heel, like a slipper.

I paused from the not inconsiderable exertion of walking

around town at a café in the square, where I took my glass
to one of the outside tables in the sunshine. Had I felt sufficiently
energetic I should have climbed up to see the castle, but since
castles do not alter much in appearance in four or five years
I shall relate what happened when I visited it the last time I
was in Mauléon.

It had been a misty morning, but the bleak grey walls of
the castle were dimly visible, looming high above the town.
I enquired about it at the grocery.

'The Château-Fort, Monsieur? Yes, it is very old, and most
interesting. There is, if you care to address yourself there, a
caretaker, who will show you round. Just follow the path that
leads off to the left of this road; it goes all the way to the top.
You will enjoy it!'

She was quite right, because as I trudged up the steep lane
that curled around the castle's hill, the mist began to lift and
shafts of pale sunshine played tentatively on the slated roofs
and turrets of the ancient houses along the lane. Soon I found
myself before the gateway to the castle. I crossed a wooden
footbridge to the huge iron-studded door and pulled an
immense bell-chain. I heard a remote clanging, some chickens
squawking, then silence. Come on, then, I thought, where's
your caretaker? Suddenly footsteps rang out behind me and
I turned to see a plain, thin woman of middle age, laden with
shopping baskets. 'No one is there, eh?' she observed, produc-
ing an enormous key and unlocking a wicket gate in the door.
This, then, was she.

'Here you are,' she said; 'there are the steps to the battlements; you can walk round while I'm putting these things
away, then I will join you.'

From the narrow parapet running round the inside of the
walls I could now see all Mauléon spread out below: there
was the Hôtel d'Andurain, there the fronton, there the Gave
and the factories. All around, now that the mist had gone, I
could see the mountains, hazy shapes walling in this lush
green valley. Away to the north they receded on both sides,
the plain widening as the Saison made its way to Sauveterre.

On a bay that was the roof of a tower lay two ancient cannon
barrels, dated 1680 and 1685, mouldering and cracking in the
grass. I walked warily along the parapet because there was no

Hôtel d'Andurain, Mauléon

handrail and I am not very good at heights. This height was
not more than fifteen feet, admittedly, and the whole of the
interior of the castle contained nothing more horrifying than
a kitchen garden, flower-beds and fruit trees, but I kept a
hand on the wall just the same. At the farthest end of the
encircling walls I peered over the edge and saw the grassy
shape of the bailey part of a motte-and-bailey castle, which
seemed to me to indicate that there had been a castle of some
kind on the site before these particular walls were built.

The caretaker now emerged from her living-quarters in the
gatehouse towers, and invited me to visit the dungeons. These
were in the gatehouse, which was well-roofed and in good
condition. She showed me a number of cells, dungeons and
oubliettes, each danker, darker and colder than the last,
without the smallest scrap of comfort for anyone unfortunate
enough to be incarcerated in them; she also gave me a good
deal of information about the castle, much of which, since
she was Polish and had a pretty dreadful accent, was incom-
prehensible. Returning from the dungeons we passed through
parts of the towers in which she actually lived (in quite a
pleasant degree of comfort), and then we were at the gates again.

'Now, Monsieur, I must go and fetch the cow.' She made
no charge and refused to take a tip. I sat outside for a while,
sketching and contemplating the creeper-grown walls and the
lazily fluttering, burbling pigeons on the roof.

Under the feudal system in the Middle Ages, a viscount,
although governing independently his own province, would be
the vassal of perhaps a stronger viscount, who in turn would
pay homage to a duke. So it came about that the Viscount of
Soule was vassal of the Viscount of Béarn, who owed allegiance
to the Duke of Gascony. For three hundred years this office
was held by the King of England.

Actual control of the domain of Gascony (or Aquitaine)
depended largely on how energetic and effectual was the
reigning king. John, Henry III and Edward II having lost
much of their French territories, Edward III and his son, the
Black Prince, set about winning them back, to extremely good
effect. After Poitiers and the Treaty of Bretigny, in 1360, the
Black Prince ruled Gascony as viceroy, and by this system of
vassalage was also Master of Soule.

Also by reason of the feudal ties, Soule as well as Béarn contrived to remain neutral throughout the greater part of the wars in France for the retention of the English kings' dominions, and by so doing prospered greatly. This came to an end when the lieutenant-general of King Charles VII of France happened to be Viscount Gaston IV of Béarn, an ambitious man who wanted the throne of Navarre. Taking advantage of the eventual defeat and exodus of the English he marched his army into Soule and occupied Mauléon (presumably holding this same castle) during the years 1449–50. Having married Princess Eleonora of Navarre, their son was obviously a claimant to the throne, and indeed was crowned King in Pamplona in 1481.

This state of Béarn-Navarre, connected by the vassal-viscounty of Soule, controlled the two principal Pyrenean passes, Roncesvalles and Somport, which should have ensured it the monopoly of Franco-Spanish trade; but trade demands peace, and since France was now united and Spain reconquered for its Catholic kings from the Moors, the preservation of Béarn-Navarre's neutrality became more and more difficult. The two great kingdoms were inclined to quarrel, and Béarn-Navarre was in the middle—described by one of its kings, Henri II, as 'a flea between two monkeys'.

Back at the Hostellerie du Château (which sported a coloured picture of the castle on all its crockery) the family of the house, Monsieur, Madame and their two pleasant-mannered sons who cooked and waited, were about to lunch. Perceiving that, although lame, I was about to load up and depart, they insisted on my taking a strengthening drink on the house. Fortified by this I set off along the road, on the other side of the Gave, almost parallel to the one by which I had arrived.

This road followed the river up its valley (which was pretty but a bit dull by Pyrenean standards) and through several villages, Libarrenx, Gotein, Menditte and so on. The houses here were quite different from those in the other Basque provinces, being Béarnais in character. They were built mainly of stone, small rounded stones from the Gave, laid together on a different slant in each alternate course, to give a herring-bone pattern. The roofs were steep, high and invariably slated.

The Church at Gotein

Farmhouses stood apart from the rest of the farm buildings instead of incorporating them, and church towers had curious three-pointed arrangements for bell-housing, known as *Trinitaires*.

The trade of slater, I imagine, must at present be one of the most prosperous in Soule, judging by the number of new roofs I saw. The steeple of the church of Troisvilles, for example, was entirely new. Troisvilles is an ordinary enough village, but it had a château and this figures as a point of interest in a story; but it belongs properly to the next chapter, so I shall deal with it later.

The afternoon's walk was really more of a shuffle and rather grim; the sun had become obscured behind a mist of cloud and the hills too had retreated out of sight. I reached Tardets at last and began the long walk along its street, past the church and the hospital and the fronton and the trinquet, and just when I thought I had run out of town, came to the square. This was surrounded on all sides by tall houses in the Souletin-Béarnais style, but typically Basque in that there were arcades all along their fronts, under the first floor. Here were shops, cafés and hotels. According to Hilaire Belloc, Tardets 'has one of the most delightful inns in all the mountains ... the "Hôtel des Pyrénées", and it is entered under the arcade of the north-west corner of the market square'.

But times change and fifty or sixty years have elapsed since Belloc wrote about it. Hôtel des Pyrénées looked to me to be in the final stages of insolvency. At the end of the same row, in the extreme north-west corner of the square, the Hôtel-Restaurant Piellenia was newer, cleaner and much more inviting, and there I stayed. My room was at the rear and had an excellent view over the Gave, up which several heroes were trying to paddle in canoes. The Gave was very swift so they were making small progress.

Down in the bar, at *l'heure de l'apéritif*, where a dozen or more local lads had gathered for the same purpose, I noticed that the walls were covered in posters advertising San Firmin. This is the annual event which, beginning traditionally on 7th July, for a week transforms Pamplona into a seething, laughing, dancing madhouse, when bars are open twenty-four hours a day and no one goes to bed; when bulls are loosed in the streets for the young braves to chase and show their mettle, and bullfights are the principal attraction. Pamplona is in Navarre, in Spain, and Tardets is in Soule, in France, but both are Basque towns and the advertisement in one for an event in the other serves even now to illustrate Basque unity: *Zazpiak Bat*; never mind France and Spain, although, as I overheard someone in Saint-Jean Pied-de-Port say when discussing San Firmin, last year there were 'more

Spaniards and Frenchmen than Basques, and more Americans than either'.

Curiously, although the Souletin architecture is the least typically Basque of all the provinces, the Souletins themselves are regarded by the rest of Eskual Herri as the most staunch Basques, preserving and practising more of the traditional songs, dances and plays than any of the others. The dances are often on the same lines as our Morris dances, and involve characters dressed in specially significant costumes; the plays are more symbolic than naturalistic, their subjects mainly biblical, historic and chivalrous. The actors psalmodize their lines, and the action is interspersed with choral singing and ballets. The folk songs, as I have previously mentioned, are really the most expressive form of Basque art; written literature is very sparse and did not exist at all prior to the sixteenth century. The first published work in Euskara was Bernard d'Etchepare's *Poésies Basques* (1545), the second a translation of the New Testament by one Leiçarraga, printed at La Rochelle in 1571 by order of the Queen of Navarre, Jeanne d'Albret, mother of Henri IV of France.

An interesting sidelight on this unshakable Basque unity was provided by a piece of wall graffiti I noticed on a barn in one of the villages along the road from Mauléon. The writer had splashed in large black letters (all dribbling a bit as usual) the words *Euzkadi Bat*: the Basque Country as One. This was not unusual: the same legend appears on walls all over the Basque Country. But either this writer or another had used the Eu of Euzkadi to add *Europa Bat*. Perhaps even the Basques are becoming less parochial these days.

Dinner at the hotel was in the kitchen, dominated by a huge fireplace and brass-embattled mantelpiece; guns hung about on the walls, the table-linen was all coloured and patterned in the traditional Basque way. Nearly every course was dressed in a tomato sauce of one kind or another, but they were all excellent and there was another interesting local cheese.

The morning was clear and fine and the view from my room was magnificent. Beyond the flashing Gave, beyond the bright trees, filling the horizon from end to end were the mountains, the proper mountains with peaks gleaming brilliant white. Well pleased with the morning and with the hotel, which was very good, I set off on the road to Oloron. My feet were still sore, but the scenery was superb and it did not seem to matter.

The Gave, or the Saison, comes down from a beautiful, lonely valley, at the far end of which is the village of Sainte-Engrace and what Belloc calls 'one of the wonders of the Pyrenees ... the gorge of the Cacouette ... a cut through the limestone such as you might make with a knife into clay or cheese, with immense steep precipices on either side.'

My road left the valley of the Saison, slid round the thickly wooded mountainside and made for a tiny village tucked away in another quiet valley called Montory. This was graced by two policemen, and automatically I felt for my passport because so far a policeman had only to see me to want to see it. But these two, obviously bored and stickily hot in the mid-day sun, and having nothing to do but watch the village girls coming out of church (it was Sunday), were content with asking me about my proposed route and recommending places (mostly, I am glad to say, already on my itinerary) which I must on no account fail to visit.

I climbed slowly and laboriously up a long, winding hill out of the silent valley. The silence, however, was shattered abruptly by the arrival, from the direction I was going, of a long concourse of cars all decorated with sundry advertising matter, the foremost of which was blaring a currently popular song from its roof-top amplifier and alternating this pleasure with blurred announcements of a trade fair in Oloron.

With this excitement over—I regret that I did not share the enthusiasm of two little boys who were picking up the copious literature thrown haphazardly at us from the car windows—its habitual placidity returned to the valley, and one could hear once more the cuckoos in the woods. At the top of the col I paused for lunch, sitting on the roadside grass in the warm sun and listening to the pleasantly rural sounds of sheep and their bells, and the birds and the breeze singing in the trees. This was the last of the Basque Country; the people in the next valley would be Béarnais and quite different. Not as obviously different as, say, an Ethiopian and an Eskimo, but different in the context of Pyreneans and their

valley communities which have remained so markedly un-
altered for so very long.

All the way from Tardets the road and I had been accompanied by the ghost of an old railway, a pair of rails mostly
half-buried beneath the tarmac, sometimes bared to the
erosive weather, usually at the side of the road. Soon after
lunch I met a farmer who was closing a gate on his sheep,
and, as he seemed disposed to chat, asked him about it. Did
it, I asked, have an engine, or were the trucks pulled by
horses?

'No, it had a steam engine, I remember it well. It ran for
about fifty years.' Belloc said that it was a tramway, which
started at Mauléon, and 'runs up the river as far as Tardets
and then turns off to the left and goes round to Oloron'. The
farmer asked me where I had been and where I was going, and
after I had told him said that he had 'been in Germany, once.
I fought with the British at Calais and Dunkirk, but then I
was captured and spent the rest of the war as a prisoner of
war. We have had enough of wars in Europe, Monsieur, we
need no more. Let us hope that we can all live in peace,
sensibly, in the future.'

We finished our conversation in amicable agreement. He
returned to his sheep, I continued down the hill, out of the
Basque Country, into Béarn.

Chapter Six

OLORON

Lanne, the first village in Béarn to which I came, appeared to be in process of being ripped apart and re-erected. The road was in tatters; hardly any of the houses were permitted to remain as they were; even the church was surrounded by scaffolding, and I could see down by the stream, which was called the Vert de Barlanes, a colony of little prefabricated cabins. I stopped for a drink in almost the only old house left unmolested; the bar-room was the downstairs living-room of a private house and was nearly as bare and primitive as Henri de Becque's, but cleaner. The old owner, in his beret and carpet slippers (in the South-West it is normal to wear one's beret indoors and one's slippers outdoors; it is not necessary to take off either), shuffled about on the bare boards and poured me some wine. Although as punctiliously polite as anyone, he was not given to conversation and, I suspect, was shy of talking with me, a monstrous mad foreigner with no hat who produced paper and wrote things down and could well have been a spy or newspaper reporter or both.

His wine was dreadful, so I had only two glasses of it.

Around a corner of the road in Lanne there appeared a gap in hills and trees and houses, and a clear sight of the Pic d'Anie, the highest mountain of the Western Pyrenees. It was entirely snow-covered, and curiously rounded like a wimpled nun peering over a crowd of brown-habited monks.

With the mountains shining in the sun on my right, and a stream splashing through pleasant woods on my left, soon I came to Aramits over a bridge across the stream. Apart from two little girls playing paleta in the fronton, the Sunday afternoon somnolence seemed to have overtaken the village. I found a splendidly decrepit hotel in a side street that dipped towards the river, and enquired for a room of a little black-dressed, greying-black-haired lady with tinted spectacles.

'We have rooms, monsieur, but they have no toilette, no cabinet, you understand.'

'Never mind about that; if you have a room, I'll take it for a night.'

There was nothing wrong with the room, except that it, in common with the entire house, had the general appearance of imminent disintegration. There were cracks in the ceiling and light-showing gaps between the floorboards. The communal lavatory and wash-place was outside, at the end of a balcony; it was certainly no worse than many I had come across. I went down to write letters in the bar, where two little girls were extracting the latest pop tunes from a juke-box, and had a brief chat with some people at the next table whose thick Béarnais accents were rather difficult to understand. I checked with them that they were in fact Béarnais—the borders of Soule were only a few miles away—and they affirmed it vigorously: 'We are all Béarnais here: you can tell by the way we talk; we laugh and enjoy life more than those gloomy Basques.'

Recalling the wedding at Santesteban I could hardly agree that the Basques were noticeably gloomy.

I had my dinner in the incredibly overcrowded little kitchen, which was evidently the nerve centre of the establishment. The whole family, papa, daughter, son-in-law (a gloomier, more saturnine character than any Basque I had come across) and two noisy little children had theirs at the next table (there were only two) and people, mainly young, drifted in and out with great frequency. For some totally illogical reason, considering the lack of space, there was a pin-ball machine by the door, the players of which completely blocked the way and had to be moved every time someone wanted to get in or out. The television was on all the time and the noise was considerable. Madame was smilingly oblivious to all this and contrived to serve a very good dinner, the main course of which was stewed hare. 'There is', she said, 'another Englishman staying in the village; I will ask him, when I see him, to come and talk with you.'

It was over my breakfast coffee in the morning (which was wet and windy) that the Englishman turned up for a chat, and it needed only a few words to establish that he was in fact an Irishman. He had married a French girl and was staying on holiday with her mother, and he was accompanied by his wife's brother-in-law, a Basque called Francis. When all this was established we had a little light conversation, and I mentioned that half the houses in Aramits and most in Lanne seemed either to be falling down or were being rebuilt.

'Oh yes,' said Tom the Irishman, 'that's because of the earthquake. Don't you remember, a couple of years ago, there was an earthquake at Arette, only a few miles from here? It caught everyone on the hop, because they'd never had one here before.'

I remembered then, and it made me think of the old curé at Vauvenargues, in Provence, whom I had met a few years before. He was of the opinion that his local hill, Sainte-Victoire, was a fragment of the Pyrenees system, long since separated from the chain by erosion and turbulence. And there had been an earthquake there, also totally unprecedented, in 1909. I thought at the time that his theory was a bit far-fetched; perhaps he was right after all.

I had intended to move on without further delay; but having met these extremely pleasant people it seemed a pity not to have further conversation with them, so I arranged with Madame Péré to stay another night and agreed to meet Tom and Francis and Tom's wife in the bar for a drink in the evening.

The only snag was that I was running short of cash, so would have to go to Oloron during the day in any case. Without much hope of a solution I called at the post office in Aramits and asked the young clerk if there was any possibility of his cashing one of my traveller's cheques. There was not, but this was a decent sort and, knowing that public transport to and from Oloron was on the scanty side, offered to take me into town that afternoon in his car.

I limped slowly around Aramits, looking at the cracked, tumbledown houses, the church stricken, closed, *interdit* and *dangereux*, and the nearby château eerily desolate, with the dark melancholy of fine buildings abandoned and empty. Also abandoned were my attempts to sketch it, because of re-curring onslaughts of drizzling rain. I bought in a chemist's some liniment and bandages for my recalcitrant feet, had some lunch at the hotel, and waited for the post office clerk, who was unnervingly late in arriving.

He was kindness itself, that young fellow. He took me to Oloron, showed me the railway station, the bus stop and the bank, and dropped me by a café so that I could wait in comfort until two o'clock, when the bank would open. The situation would have been excellent in every way but for the rain, which now fell steadily with an air of permanence. However, there were things to see in Oloron, and after visiting the Bank of France, whose staff were charming, cheerful and courteous, I began by climbing up the steep hill between the two rivers to the old church of Sainte-Croix.

The rivers, the Gaves d'Aspe and d'Ossau, meet a little below the town and form the Gave d'Oloron, and it was on this strategically useful hill between the V-shaped confluence that one of Caesar's officers, Publius Crassus, in the year 56 B.C., having passed through the Somport pass in the mountains with his army, established a base. This camp became a town, called Illuro, and the capital of the tribe in whose territory it was situated. These were known by the Romans as the Civitas Elloronensium, one of the Nine Peoples. Since the road over the Somport to Sarragossa was one of the principal Pyrenean passes, the commanding position of Illuro occasioned its importance, and the town flourished. When the Roman Empire became officially Christian the first of the local bishoprics were gradually established, and in due course Illuro became the seat of one Gratus, subsequently canonized. His presence at the Council of Agde was recorded in 506. Tucked away in a corner of Gaul, the town did not attract too much attention from the waves of Vandals, Visigoths and Franks who swept across Europe and precipitated the decline, if not the fall, of the Roman Empire; but its position made it an obvious target for the Saracens, who came the other way out of Spain. Abd el Rahman's hordes sacked it in 732. But it was the Normans, a hundred or so years after that, who finally demolished the old town. They came from the north, followed the Adour and the Gaves and, like the aesthetic, intelligent and philanthropic colonizers that they were, destroyed everything in their path. Illuro ceased to exist in 843, and it was two hundred years before anyone had an impulse constructive enough to revive it; this hero was Centulle V, Viscount of Béarn.

The viscounty of Béarn had developed from two very small areas, the valley of the Gave de Pau in the vicinity of Lescar, which also had a Roman bishop, and the country around Morlaas called Vic-Bilh. Having been known in Nine Peoples days as Civitas Benarnensium, from Beneharnum, the old name of Lescar, the names were sensibly contracted and shortened to Béarn, and during the ninth century, while the Normans were spreading their unenlightened creed across the land, the first viscounts emerged.

The energy of Centulle V, in 1080, created the *For d'Oloron*, the oldest municipal charter in France, founded the church of Sainte-Croix and installed in it a bishop once again. Also he united Oloron and the three Pyrenean valleys it commanded with his viscounty, and within this framework and beneath the rule of successive viscounts the city continually prospered.

Climbing up the steep little street towards Sainte-Croix I noticed on the right a solitary and obviously ancient tower, which appears to be all that is left of the former bishops' palace and is called Tour de Grède. Several bits of the old walls and ramparts crop up here and there in this ancient quarter, the original site of the town, and the houses are worth a whole collection of sketches. (It was still raining, so someone else will have to make the collection, if he has not done so already.) Considering its nine hundred years, it is surprising, not that Sainte-Croix has been restored and altered and patched up from time to time, but that any of the original structure remains. The guide-book writer of the Syndicat d'Initiative says that 'the visitor will remark the unity of style, the harmonious proportions of this Roman edifice' (he means Roman in style) 'and the severity, the nobility of its lines, which will impose on his memory'. True, but the visitor will be less impressed than he ought to be because of the difficulty of seeing anything at all inside; there are hardly any windows, so the interior is cavernous, gloomy and dark.

Outside, a terrace has been constructed so that from Sainte-Croix, the very top of the town, one can see, again to quote the guide-book, 'one of the finest spectacles which one may have of the Pyrenees'. The jumbled mass of precipitous snowy peaks range in confusion, one after another, in endless procession across the horizon. But 'the clearest and softest of lights

Sainte-Croix, Oloron

of the blue sky which can give free course to poetic inspiration' was not, that afternoon, too apparent. The sky was a sombre, lowering blue-grey and the mountains looked icy cold and terrifyingly forbidding.

In a square behind and below Sainte-Croix, Place Saint-

Pierre, is another church, of the name of the square. It was used, when I walked past it, as a garage, because it had long been 'disaffected'.

Rue Labarraque, named after a celebrated physicist who was born in one of the old houses, led me steeply back down towards the Gave d'Aspe. The houses on both sides were aged, some with overhanging first storeys and by no means as well preserved as the chemist's birth place. Those on the Gave side must surely fall into it sooner or later.

Across the Gave d'Aspe is the twin town of Sainte-Marie, which until 1858 had a separate corporate existence. I walked up Rue de Révol to its cathedral which, although it looks of a different age than Sainte-Croix, was in fact begun only twenty years or so later. The Viscount then was Gaston IV, a man with a reputation for high chivalry and integrity, who spent many years fighting the enemies of Christianity in the Holy Land and in Spain. On returning from the former campaign he inaugurated the foundation of the cathedral, the porch of which is still much the same as it was then (allowing for wear and tear). It is an elaborately decorated rounded Romanesque arch in a similar style (and of the same period) as those of Saint-Gilles and Arles, in Provence, and from that resemblance could even have been the work of the same sculptor, one Brunus. The doorway is divided by a supporting column whose caryatids look like chained, imprisoned Saracens —possibly a reference to the Viscount's campaign—and immediately above it is a representation in bas-relief of the Descent from the Cross. On the two semi-circular outer rims of the arch, in minute detail, are figurines depicting the vision of Saint John and the twenty-four Elders of the Apocalypse, playing sundry musical instruments. Surmounting columns to right and left of the porch are, respectively, a mounted knight whose face, either through vandalism or the elements, has lost all its features but who presumably represented Viscount Gaston IV, and a lion or monster with, surprisingly, a man disappearing head first into its mouth.

The interior of the cathedral, allowing for the murky light of the afternoon, was nearly as dark as Sainte-Croix; but there was enough light for me to see some more sculptures, showing the miracles of St Gratus, the first Elloronean bishop, and in the choir near the altar the unmistakable outlines of a Chippendale chair.

The only bus back to Aramits appeared to run at an hour which would make me quite certain to arrive too late for dinner, let alone a drink with the Irish-Béarnais-Basque federation, so after a ruminative beer in the bus-stop café and a look at a copy of *Sud-Ouest*, which turned out to be the sporting edition and had no other kind of news, I decided to try to hitch-hike back. I found the road without any difficulty and within quite a short time was picked up by an Aramits man who had been drinking in the bar of Hotel Péré yesterday and recognized me.

Irish Tom, his French wife Lily and her Basque brother-in-law Francis duly turned up and a three-cornered conversation ensued, because Tom spoke very little French and Francis about as much English, so Lily and I translated for both. The conversation was fairly general, about the effects of the Arette earthquake and how worried they were for Lily's mother, and about prices in France compared with England, and about the potentialities of Europe's future which Francis, a *maître d'hôtel* in Paris, thought would be complicated by language difficulties more than anything else. One point of interest, however, that did emerge was Lily's assertion that Dumas's character Aramis, one of the Three Musketeers, was a real person and was born in the château here in Aramits, from which his name derived.

When a novelist uses an historic person as a character and twists him to suit his story it is often extremely difficult to sort out what is fact and what fiction. Even when there is no basis at all for believing a character to have existed, some people will believe that he did; there are those in England who will show you, with enough circumstantial detail to convict the most devious of felons, a house lived in and articles used by someone who lived only in an author's mind. While perfectly willing to believe Lily's claim I was yet a little dubious, because I had always thought the Musketeers were fictitious and because I wondered if she might be repeating one of those local beliefs based on similarity of names.

The facts, as usual, are a compromise. Dumas, in his preface to *The Three Musketeers*, says that he based his story on a manuscript published at the beginning of the eighteenth century, entitled *Mémoires de Monsieur d'Artagnan*, who was in fact a captain in the King's Musketeers during the reign of King Louis XIII, and that, in this narrative, 'd'Artagnan relates that on his first visit to M. de Tréville, Captain of the Royal Musketeers, he met three young men in the ante-chamber, serving in the illustrious corps into which he solicited the honour of being admitted, and bearing the names of Athos, Porthos, and Aramis'. While searching for further historical matter on which to base his story Dumas found the *Mémoires de M. le Comte de la Fère*, which was the title eventually admitted to by Athos in the book, and in its pages he discovered the names of all three Musketeers.

All very convincing; but Dumas had a habit of altering facts and dates in history to suit his story. In *The Three Musketeers* the events run continuously, from the Duke of Buckingham's flirtation with the Queen to the siege of La Rochelle and his assassination. In fact, three years separated the affair of Queen Anne of Austria and the siege of La Rochelle, and there appears to be no evidence of the Musketeers' part in either episode.

But there is no reason why the names of these men should not have been those of real men. D'Artagnan 'made every effort to find out who Athos, Porthos and Aramis really were; for under one of those assumed appellations, each of these young men concealed his real name'. And although 'M. de Troisville, as his family was yet called in Gascony', was admitted also to be a Gascon, in fact they all were.

During the sixteenth and seventeenth centuries the population of Béarn expanded, and, as happens in small countries with large populations, it became commonplace for young men to leave home and seek their fortunes in other lands. Several young Béarnais of good family—rich merchant class— went to Paris and took arms for the King. One of these was Isaac de Portau of Pau (Porthos), another was Armand de Sillègue d'Autevielle (Athos), and yet another, Henri, the lay abbé of Aramits (Aramis). Captain de Tréville was in fact Lord of the Manor of Troisville, through which I had passed a day or two before. And since d'Artagnan's father told him about 'M. de Tréville, once my neighbour', we can suppose that his family were also Souletins.

So Henri d'Aramits the Musketeer existed; but Aramis the Musketeer who helped to preserve the good name of Anne d'Autriche (which by all accounts was non-existent: gossip of *l'affaire Buckingham* was widespread) was the sole property of Alexandre Dumas.

Despite hot water and salts very kindly provided in the morning by Madame Péré, who could not have been more solicitous on my behalf, my ease of movement was still more like that of an arthritic robot than a Pyrenean walker, so another change of plans had to be contemplated. At this rate I could do only about twelve or thirteen kilometres a day, quite inadequate to cover in the time the distance I had intended to travel. Progress would therefore have to be made, regrettably enough and with callous disregard of my walking reputation, by public transport and by Rule of Thumb (a euphemism for begging free rides in other people's cars). It would still, most likely, involve a fair amount of walking, since I wanted to go to Lourdes by a mountainous route, and motorists generally did not seem to share this preference.

Salt-bathed, anointed and bandaged, I said good-bye to Madame Péré, who almost cried, and left Aramits on the road to Oloron. I thumbed a lift from a man who dropped me on the outskirts, by which time it had started to rain again. I made for the station, meeting on the way a man who was mad or drunk or both. I ignored him, but he kept saying, 'Are you afraid of me, hein? Eh? Uh?', and wanted me to join him in a drink. When I refused he became abusive. The rain was hammering down and I got annoyed and shouted a very rude word in Anglo-Saxon at him as he made for his favourite (and dingy) bistro. I reached the station and had an hour in which to wait and dry off.

Although the railway penetrated the Val d'Ossau as far as Laruns, the train did not; at Buzy one boarded (actually three did, not counting the driver) a large motor-coach run by the S.N.C.F., which performed the function of the train. The rain lashed down, the slate-roofed villages, Arudy,

Izeste, Bielle, came and went and soon I was standing in the square at Laruns. It was about lunch time; perhaps if I waited an hour or so the rain would stop. I lurched into the nearest hotel and ordered bread, cheese and beer.

Chapter Seven

PILGRIMAGE OF A HERETIC

While the daughter of the *patronne* of the hotel I had chosen fetched for me a colossal slab of cheese and half a loaf which she insisted was a sandwich, her mother, a plump, blonde lady, sat in the bar-room and read the newspapers. Having eaten as much as I could of that monstrous creation (for which they charged me five shillings) I rose and peered out at the unchanged outdoor scene: thick grey- clouds cloaking the mountains and persistent, relentless rain. 'It does not', I commented to Madame, who was sitting near, 'look at all promising.'

'It will certainly rain all day,' she said complacently but with an effort at commiseration; 'it always does when it's like this. Where are you going?'

'Lourdes, by way of the mountains. I want to go up to Eaux Bonnes and over the Col d'Aubisque.'

'Col d'Aubisque? But I believe that it is not passable for motor traffic yet.'

'I am on foot.'

'Then you might possibly get through; but there is a danger of rocks falling on the road, you understand, because of the rain and the melting snow. If you were to enquire at one of the hotels in Gourette, which is just this side of the Col, they would tell you if one is permitted to proceed.'

'But if one is not,' I observed, 'then I should have to come all the way back, which would be tiresome for one on foot and afflicted with a *mal-à-pied*. Is there no other way from here to Lourdes?'

'But certainly, if one goes down the valley to Louvie-Juzon. But why not stay in Laruns, Monsieur? It is a pleasant and interesting old town.'

At present I should have to take her word for that, since it would be impossible to take more than half a dozen paces

102

without getting drenched. The weather, God's curse on it, was preventing me from savouring the (admittedly arduous) pleasures of walking in the High Pyrenees. If it was going to rain for the rest of the day (which it did) I might as well stay put. 'Have you a room here, Madame?'

'Certainly. I think you would be wise not to go any farther today, Monsieur.'

Marie, the daughter, showed me the room; in it was a wooden bedside lamp in the shape of a bear. 'You see this? It is a Pyrenean bear.'

'Are there still', I asked, 'bears in the mountains?'

'Oh, yes. In the Reserve Naturelle d'Ossau there are fifty at least.'

This surprised me, because I had heard that the Pyrenean bears were practically extinct. But the Nature Reserve on the foothills of the Pic du Midi d'Ossau, a higher mountain than Pic d'Anie, had long been established and the bears could have regenerated. I should have to enquire further.

There was nothing I could do but sit in the hotel, read, write and snooze, listen to the sheep and cows being driven wetly across the square (in the middle of which, incongruously, a fountain played), to the church bell chiming in a peculiarly unco-ordinated fashion, to the monotonous beating of a million raindrops a second. And to a sing-song which seemed to be developing downstairs around a honky-tonk piano which stood in the hall. When I descended for an aperitif the group of boys who had been thus filling in time were now playing records on Marie's gramophone. She, a tall, bony lady of perhaps thirty, told me that the boys, although decent enough, were all out of work and would spend hours in the hotel bar over one drink each, and make a lot of noise in the process.

There hung on the wall of the bar-restaurant the stuffed head of a species of deer, with straight horns hooked over backwards at the top. I had an idea that this might be an izard, and asked the only other resident about it, an elderly lady in black, at dinner.

'Yes,' she said, 'there are plenty of izards in the mountains. Only last week an izard leapt out in the road in front of a motorist, an unfortunate woman who swerved and precipitated herself into a ravine, which killed her.'

'What about bears?'

'Bears, yes, there are bears—I think.' She turned to one of the boys, who had produced some money and was treating his pals to brandy. 'Do you know if there are still bears?'

The boy, flushed and a little drunk, glanced from the lady to me, and a sneer crept into his countenance.

'Bears? Oh yes, plenty of fierce bears. Monsieur is afraid of going up the road in case of being eaten by bears?'

'But of course,' I said mildly. 'I'm terrified.'

Another of the boys laughed and gave his friend a push. 'Don't mind him, Monsieur. Yes, there are some bears in the Reserve Naturelle, but not very many. There are plenty of izards and wild boars, however, and other small kinds of animals, and birds. Eagles, too.'

'Yes, that is right,' said the lady in black; 'there are eagles, which sometimes steal the young lambs.'

This conversation was the nearest I got to the wild life of the mountains. I had originally intended to go and see the Reserve Naturelle for myself, but the two recurring problems of this expedition, the weather and my *mal-à-pied*, combined to prevent me. I had even made a note of Belloc's advice on how best to find it. After passing through Eaux Chaudes, 'a dismal place, squeezed in between the torrent and the cliff, dirty, uncomfortable and sad', one advanced up the narrow, deep valleys to Gabas, 'which may be said to consist in three inns, a ruinous chapel, most pathetic, and a customs station', and then one approaches the mighty and awe-inspiring Pic du Midi. 'This ascent by the short valley from Gabas, through the woods, is better, because you come right up on to the mountain suddenly from the depth of a vast forest, and you feel its isolation.' I had wanted to experience this isolation, sit for an hour or two in it, maybe, and if I were to be quiet and still enough, perhaps catch a glimpse of some of the shy creatures which live in it. But creatures, however shy, were not likely to want to risk pneumonia by venturing out in the rain any more than I did.

Eaux Chaudes, so despised by Belloc, is a thermal station, and so is Eaux Bonnes, on the other road, the one up to the Col d'Aubisque. They were made popular in the first instance by a Béarnais called Théophile de Bordeu, whose life-span covered three-quarters of the eighteenth century. He was known as 'the Voltaire of Medicine' because he fought all his life for a more scientific approach to medicine. He had great faith in the curative properties of the thermal waters of the Pyrenees, and as he was a powerful writer he was able to influence his contemporaries to the extent of encouraging them to go to the stations and take the waters.

The morning was cloudy, but dry. It was still impossible to see the Pic du Midi, which was a great pity (I wanted at least to sketch it from the Val d'Ossau), but one could at last venture out of doors without fear of drowning. The bill at the hotel, I thought, was rather excessive, but even then it was very modest compared with the kind of thing one can encounter in French hotels if one is incautious enough to pick the glossier, more *touristique* variety.

I started walking down the valley road back the way the bus had come yesterday. I could now see my surroundings more clearly, and could admire the peaceful green quiet of it, the little grey villages with old churches and farmhouses, the steep pine-covered mountainsides. One would not have thought it of two of the villages, so immutably rustic in appearance, but in the sixteenth century, under the aegis of King Henri II d'Albret of Béarn-Navarre, Béon and Aste became iron-mining centres. It was remarkably like the situation in the Weald of Kent and Sussex, where at about the same time delightful villages such as Lamberhurst, Horsmonden and Ashburnham became a clanging, smoking, sulphurous black country in the same interests.

After about an hour's walking I was given a lift the rest of the way down the valley to Louvie-Juzon, past a little castle on a rock in the middle of the valley. I took the road to Lourdes, and it led to the centre of the village where the queer old stone church stood, with a conical stone steeple, and up a violently steep and twisting road (which was being repaired: like walking on Brighton beach) round the corner of the mountainside.

The country into which I now came was a very lonely, sequestered valley, far less populous than the Val d'Ossau, with no villages and few farms. The woods were thick on all sides, sheep grazed the lush pastures; the only sounds that drifted on the air were their bells, the song of birds and the occasional splash of a hillside stream. There was hardly any traffic, either, only four or five vehicles in an hour, and they were vans or lorries. Eventually (the sun was now shining and if I had been less afflicted of foot I should have declined it) I was given a lift by a family of three, Papa, Maman and teenage daughter, beside whom I squeezed in the back. Papa was a sensible motorist who trundled gently along those narrow winding lanes and appreciated the scenery. We followed the remainder of this wonderfully lovely valley, through its only two villages, until the country flattened out and we came to Bruges. 'Aha,' said Papa, 'we have lost our way, and are now in Belgium!'

On the way to the Nationale 637, which would take me direct to Lourdes, we passed notices at the roadside which Papa read out for the family's instruction. 'Grottes de Betharram: Son et Lumière, Musique et Histoire. We shall certainly pay them a visit.' On the Nationale they stopped in the town of Lestelle-Betharram, and said they were going to find somewhere for lunch. Quite why I did not follow their example I do not know. I pressed on, out of the town, past a large convent-cum-hospital by the Gave de Pau, on a long straight stretch of the Nationale. Everyone else was at lunch and I should have known that this would be the case. I walked to within about a kilometre of the Grottes, which were screened by an entrance foyer building at the foot of the soaring mountains, with the Gave tumbling and foaming down below, and then was lucky. A very pleasant young man with some English pulled up alongside me, and a quarter of an hour and some light conversation later I was standing in the middle of Lourdes.

There was no problem of finding an hotel in Lourdes, because it was quite difficult to find a house which was not one. This made me deeply suspicious of all of them, and brought to mind Belloc's gloomy assessment, that Lourdes, 'like all cosmopolitan towns, is detestable in its accommodation, and to make it the more detestable there is that admixture of the supernatural which is invariably accompanied by detestable earthly adjuncts'. Belloc himself was a Catholic, so if he thought this, what would a heretic Anglican find? There was,

The Castle of Lourdes

at any rate, no shortage of choice. Ignoring his further advice
to 'avoid the hotels that have Holy names to them, they are
usually frauds', I chose a small terraced house in the square
by the baths and near the Post Office, called Hôtel Saint-Yves.
I was greeted, when I stepped inside, by a tall, thin and
young version of M. Etchandy of Saint-Jean Pied-de-Port,
who seemed at once cheerful and business-like, and not at all
likely to be a fraud. The room was the statutory two floors up,
small, clean, comfortable, and overlooking the square. It all
seemed highly satisfactory, so I set off to inspect the town.

Lourdes has acquired an 'odour of sanctity' during the last
hundred years, since, according to the New Roman Missal,
'between 11th February and 16th July 1858 the Blessed
Virgin appeared eighteen times to Bernadette Soubirous, the

fourteen-year-old shepherdess, in a grotto of the rock of Massabielle at Lourdes'. But the town was important, for a different reason, long before that: it was, and is, dominated by a large and solidly built stone castle on a high outcrop of rock exactly where the Gave de Pau emerges from its Pyrenean valley and bends sharply around the base of the rock before continuing to Pau, Orthez and the Adour. Although the castle has not, by virtue of Béarn's long neutrality which Bigorre shared, a long history of siege and sortie, it was nevertheless important strategically and still presents an impressive spectacle. Bigorre, of which Lourdes is a principal town, corresponds more or less with the territory occupied by the Bigerriones, one of the Nine Peoples, and is nowadays in the Département of Hautes-Pyrénées.

That Lourdes owes much to young Saint Bernadette is evident the moment one arrives in the place: the streets nearer to the Grotto make it blatantly obvious. They are lined on both sides with countless shops, all selling an incredible assortment of vulgar, tasteless and totally unpleasant curios and souvenirs and otherwise unsaleable objects which could not justify more fully Belloc's description of 'detestable earthly adjuncts'. Canterbury must have been similarly afflicted in Chaucer's day. Emerging, with considerable relief, from these chambers of horrors, I came to the gardens which are laid out around the Basilica which had been built over the Grotto in the rock of Massabielle. A number of people, including numerous priests, nurses and nuns, were gathering, and when I reached the area in front of the Basilica I found that a tremendous concourse was gathered and a service was in progress, relayed by loud-speaker. The more able members of the congregation crowded all the staircases and galleries around the front of the Basilica, and in the basin immediately before it were ranks of invalid chairs, all occupied. A priest was chanting, the people responding, musically, with a re-iterated 'Vive Jésus, vive sa Croix'. Many other invalids, with sticks and crutches, were present, but this was only the beginning of the pilgrim season and nothing like the crowds that would later develop and fill the multitudinous hotels and patronize the Rubbish Shops.

But it would be unfair to stress the 'detestable earthly

At the Basilica, Lourdes

adjuncts' to Lourdes. The essence of Lourdes, which was apparent to me in a diluted form, is faith; a friend, Giles Champion, encountered it at its fullest pitch in the summer of 1967, and here is what he wrote of it:

'We arrived in Lourdes with the dusk, and parked the car on a hill alongside the Basilica. As we moved out to the terrace we could both feel that something was about to happen: thousands of people were milling around in the square below and more poured in every minute. Below us along the sheer, rugged side of the Basilica more people were filling containers with the holy water.

'As we came down from the terrace and joined the crowds, the feeling of intense reverence and faith seemed to envelop us; nuns, priests, nurses and the masses jostled against each other. We realized that this was the end of a pilgrimage for Catholics from all nations.

'As we walked past the stream of holy water by the Basilica we could hear Mass being chanted through loud-speakers and responses taken up by the thousands of pilgrims. We came to the shrine set in two caves in the walls of the Basilica: in one were masses of many-sized candles all burning brightly (the roof of the cave was blackened by soot) and high up there hung rows of crutches and walking-sticks. In the other cave, although we could not quite see, pilgrims seemed to be filing through to kiss the shrine.

'Suddenly all was quiet: then a choir of small boys on the lower steps of the Basilica began to sing the *Ave Maria*, quite alone, uninterrupted. Then the voices of the pilgrims joined in. The candles they had been carrying were lit and a procession formed, in their native groups: they moved from the shrine, around the gentle curve of the terrace, down to the square, right up one side of the gardens and down the other, coming eventually to a halt in the square before the Basilica; all the while they sang the *Ave Maria*.

'We walked up the gardens against the flow of the procession: neither of us had ever felt or seen before such an incredible expression of faith. The whole torchlit procession wound relentlessly on and shadowy, flickering faces sang for faith and marvellous adoration.'

Even if one has not come to Lourdes as a pilgrim the town

is still extremely well worth staying in (if averting one's eyes from the aforesaid adjuncts) because of its position. The mountains, the high town of Argelès-Gazost, the beautiful wild High Pyrenees and the roads to Cauterets, Luz and Gavarnie are all eminently accessible, and the kind of hotel in which I stayed was remarkably inexpensive (room and dinner for about thirty shillings) and not in the least detestable.

My company for dinner consisted of the owner, an elderly lady, and the staff, because I was the only resident. After they had dined, the pretty blonde wife of the tall man produced a cake, and a bottle of white Jurançon wine, and said 'Vive Saint-Georges'. I, as an Englishman, echoed this because it was his day, but observed that although he was our patron saint we did not, and perhaps ought to, have some special cake or dish to commemorate him. 'This cake isn't specially for Saint George,' she said, 'but it is rather nice. Would you like to try it?' Her husband gave me a drop of the sweet white Jurançon to taste with it, and we talked of food and wine and the inevitable *oui* and *non* talks on the television until I went to bed.

As I made my slow, painful, crustacean way out of town in the morning (which was warm and dry but not sunny) I reflected that even if I had a walking stick there would not have been much point in leaving it at the shrine of Saint Bernadette. But there is more than one kind of miracle, and mine came when, having gained the road to Pau (the same by which I had arrived the day before) and waved my thumb in that essential but rather undignified way that indicates to motorists that one would appreciate a lift, the third car so signalled stopped and its occupant offered one. He was a good-looking and neatly dressed young Spaniard from Barcelona, living at Bordes, near Pau, and was going there now. He happened also to be a devout Christian. 'Catholic?' I asked. 'Evangelist,' he said. A text from one of the Gospels was taped to his dashboard, and he showed me a small bible tucked into one of the glove compartments. 'One can do just so much in life,' he said, 'using one's own judgment. But there comes a time when God's guidance is essential.' He tapped the bible. 'Don't you find that, on your travels?'

'Well, I don't carry a bible around with me,' I said, 'but I must say, difficulties are more easily overcome with a little faith. Like today, for example. . . .'

'Exactly. I do not normally take many hitch-hikers, because many are not at all pleasant types of person. But I saw that you were afflicted of the foot and patently honest and so I stopped.' He chatted on in a way that few even of the most earnest evangelists would have dared to, in England, with a complete stranger, but he was not trying to preach.

The country, the wide flat valley of the Gave de Pau, was rather dull. When we reached Bordes, where the Spaniard had a house, a wife and six children, he did not stop but took me on to Pau, ten kilometres farther.

Chapter Eight

THE TREASURES OF PAU

The Spaniard dropped me by the railway station at Pau, which when constructed rather spoilt what Lamartine called 'the finest view from the land, as Naples is the finest from the sea'. The town, dominated by the castle, stands on a hill above the Gave de Pau and looks across the green foothills to the continuously changing backdrop of the Pyrenees. The changes, not perhaps immediately expected of immovable objects like mountains, are worked by light and shadow, sunshine and cloud; the day I arrived in Pau the clouds had succeeded in changing them so much I could not see them at all.

Having originally planned to stay a couple of nights in Pau, the better to explore the place, I went to Jurançon, across the Gave from Pau, where there was a good inn in which I had stayed before. The same people, expatriates from Algeria, were there, but they had no rooms spare, so I retraced my way back across the bridge, up into the town. For some reason I managed to pick all the streets where there were no hotels and thus spent hours and a lot of energy trailing round looking for one. I drew several blanks, even after directions from an extremely voluble but nevertheless helpful lady whom I met near the market place, and eventually came to roost in a place called 'L'As de Trèfle' quite some way out of town. It was not brilliant: it had no restaurant and little else besides a scruffy bar, and the people were inclined to indifference, but by this time I was in no mood to look for another.

Feeling tidier, cleaner and refreshed I ventured out a little while later in the mild sunshine which was now beginning to break through, back into town to visit the castle. In the quarter in which this stood I discovered all the small hotels I had been looking for. I bought two tickets, one for the castle and one for the Béarnais Museum housed in it, and

The Castle of Pau

waited in a sort of foyer for a guide, with a dozen and a half other people.

I went first to the castle because it is both the nucleus of the town and the repository of most of its history. Like many castles, the present structure was not the first built on the site; there had been fortifications of some sort there since those dim unrecorded centuries of Béarnais history. Basically, the building in which I was sitting, listening to the chatter of the French school-children guarded by a nun, and the terse, phlegmatic utterances of an elderly couple who could not have been (and were not) anything else but English, was erected as part of a defence plan by Viscount Gaston III of Béarn, he who was called Gaston Phoebus. The huge tower, near which one enters the courtyard, was built of brick, a relatively new technique of construction in the fourteenth century.

The worth and wisdom of Gaston Phoebus as ruling viscount of his small domain lay in his ability to appreciate the value of building up a large, efficient army and redoubtable fortresses for defence purposes only. Many rulers, having begun this way, have been unable to resist the temptation to use the army for foreign conquests, but Gaston had no ambition other than to provide stable rule, justice and, above all, peace for his country. He was in fact outstanding more as a diplomat and administrator than as a warrior, and he was, for a four-teenth-century ruler, remarkably moderate. His access of choler at his son's obstinacy, which led to the latter's death at Orthez, was an isolated, if tragic, instance: he seldom con-demned any offender to death, and even prison sentences were for justly proved crimes. That his benign but firm system of rule was justified is proved by the result: under it his subjects enjoyed total peace.

The guide arrived, a small dapper man with the valuable talent of saying his lines about each successive object of interest on the tour clearly, slowly and distinctly and with neither emotion nor boredom. He led us through the fine rooms, beautifully preserved and restored, pointed out the furniture—'armchair, Louis XIII, writing-table, Louis XV, chimney-breast and fireplace, Henri IV'—and explained why, in the lower staircase and in one of the magnificent rooms, the ceiling was decorated with the letters H and M.

King Henri II d'Albret, of Béarn-Navarre, married Marguerite d'Angoulême, who was a princess of the French Royal house. Finding that the Castle of Orthez was much too chilly and uncomfortable for so delicately nurtured a lady, he had the Castle of Pau altered and enlarged, with fine rooms, terraces and huge windows, all in the elegant, classical renaissance style. This work lasted from 1529 to 1535, and it transformed an equally uncomfortable fortress into a magnificent royal palace. Despite this the Queen was not fond of it and rarely stayed there, but it had the effect of increasing the importance of Pau and in fact Henri II made it his capital.

He was the most outstanding ruler of Béarn since Gaston Phoebus, and in many ways his efforts were parallel to those of his predecessor. He reorganized his country's defence system, its legal system, its financial arrangements and practically all branches of its economy. Agriculture, still the principal livelihood of the Béarnais, needed developing: Henri encouraged farmers from other parts of France to settle in Béarn and teach its peasants other arts than their traditional pasturage and stock-breeding. The vineyards of Jurançon and Monein began to flourish. He encouraged also other industries: the iron-mines of the valleys of Ouzon and Ossau opened; but it was the textile industry that was the most important innovation, particularly at Oloron.

Although not universally successful, since human nature being for ever obdurate many of the peasant workers refused to abandon methods which were good enough for father, grandfather and Adam, the efforts of Henri II d'Albret created in Béarn an oasis of peace and industry in an increasingly violent and disrupted France.

On another floor were the sumptuous apartments occupied by Napoleon III and the Empress Eugénie, the last crowned heads to rest in the castle. The rooms had been restored to their original splendour, the furniture re-upholstered in glowing brocades, the carpets deep, the chairs and tables shining.

For all his rather contrived imperial splendour, which evaporated as soon as Bismarck pricked the bubble, Louis-Napoleon was not much of a character. Greater by far, as a man, a personality and a real king, was Henri IV. Another room in the castle was his birthplace, and in it was the huge tortoise-shell they used as his cradle. Also present were sundry of his relics and a surprising number of statues, busts and portraits of him. A great king by any standards, he could have been greater still if circumstances had allowed him to be born at a different date and to a less bigoted mother. Gaston Phoebus and Henri II d'Albret were both far more beneficial to Béarnais peace and prosperity, but then they had not to cope with the whole of France, divided and torn between mutually destructive raving fanatics. Henri IV, 'Noustre Henric', is far too rich a character to dismiss in a paragraph and I shall tell more of him a little later.

The last item in the guided tour was the most impressive; all those lovely things that we had seen, the period furniture, the silver candelabra, the delicate Sèvres china, the rich and luxurious draperies, hangings and panellings, the Royal Navarrese cradle, all were treasures of a kind, but the real treasures of Pau are the tapestries.

As a collection of tapestries (they date from the fifteenth to the seventeenth century) they are remarkable enough; but their quality puts them in a class with the most celebrated paintings, sculptures, engravings or carvings. Their subjects are various. There are several series, of the seasons of the year and their appropriate rural activities, of the mythical visit of Psyche to Ceres, of the life and death of St John the Baptist, of great castles and mansions in the fair land of France and of scenes of the favourite mediaeval sport of princes, the Chase. The guide limited his discourse to explaining the nature of each work and its age. There was no need to say more, the tapestries spoke for themselves. Here is what Dornford Yates wrote of them:

'Standing before those aged exquisites—those glorious embodiments of patience infinite, imagination high, and matchless craftsmanship, I forgot everything. The style of them was superb. They had quality. About them was nothing mean. They were so rich, so mellow, so delicate. There was a softness to the lovely tones no brush could ever compass. Miracles of detail, marvels of stately effect, the panels were breathing the spirit of their age. Looking upon them, I stepped into another world. I heard the shouts of the huntsmen and the laughter of the handmaidens, I smelled the sweat of the chargers and the sweet scent of the grapes, I felt the cool touch of the shade upon my cheeks. Always the shouts were distant, the scent faint, the laughter low. I wandered up faery glades, loitered in lazy markets, listened to the music of fountains, sat before ample boards, bowed over lily-white hands. . . .

'Here, then, was magic. Things other than silk went to the weaving of so potent a spell. The laborious needle put in the dainty threads: the hearts of those that plied it put in most precious memories—treasures of love and laughter . . . the swift brush of lips . . . the echo of a call in the forest . . . a patch of sunlight upon the slope of a hill . . . such stuff, indeed, as dreams are made on. . . .'

From the transcendent to the prosaic one took the next staircase to the third floor of the castle and visited the Béarnais Museum. Facts are such stuff as museums are made on, and this one is so full of them that, if a person was eager to learn anything whatever of Béarn, here would be the place to search for it. Here is a collection of natural curiosities, cases full of butterflies, stuffed izards, eagles, vultures, a huge and somewhat off-putting stuffed bear, an array of antique agricultural implements and details of how they were used, information on local soldiers, writers, poets and artists, with specimens of their work, and a wealth of Béarnais history and culture. I was still studying some of this, having had to skip much of it, when the man in charge of it came to see what I was doing. He seemed relieved to find that I had neither died in some distant gallery nor was engaged in pocketing the sickles and bagging-hooks, and gathering that I was just interested proceeded to tell me all the things I had just found out (from reading the totally explicit labels) for myself.

The sun was shining quite warmly when I left the castle, so I went and idled on the terrace in front of it, overlooking the Gave (and the railway station). There was no sign of the mountains, which was a pity, but there was no rain either and for that I was extremely grateful. I walked about the streets for a while, passing in one a house draped with a Swedish flag. This was the birthplace of Jean-Baptiste Bernadotte, one of those young Béarnais who sought and found fame and fortune outside his native land. He joined the army in 1780, became an adjutant in 1790, and then the Revolutionary wars swept him to prominence. In 1794 he was general of a division, and his success encouraged numbers of his compatriot Béarnais to follow him in the Napoleonic wars. He was made Marshal of the Empire, and then, almost by mistake, was asked to be crown prince, and subsequently king, of Sweden.

In Place Clémenceau, a spacious square in the fashionable centre of the town, I found an agreeable café and sat at one of its outside tables, sipping iced pastis and watching Palois life going by. Actually Pau is not as fashionable now as it was in the nineteenth century, when it sprouted quite a sizeable English colony. It started when some of Wellington's ex-officers, remembering the mildness of the climate, the beauty of the scenery and the kindness of the people, decided to return to Pau, and having done so, stayed. One of the first, a retired Indian Army officer called Bunbury, apparently regretted staying because his daughter fell in love with and wanted to marry the poet Alfred de Vigny. Bunbury was one of those die-hards who think that anyone who writes poetry must be soft, gutless and possibly also not quite nice, and made a great show to his friends of being unable to remember his son-in-law's name. If this is true he must have been singularly bigoted, because de Vigny was a soldier too and had been garrisoned in Béarn since 1823. He married Bunbury's daughter in 1825.

The colony flourished, especially when Dr Alexander Taylor published, in 1842, a paper on *The Curative Influence of the Climate of Pau*, and Thermalism, the hobby-horse ridden so many years before by Théophile de Bordeu, came into its own: delicate constitutions by the hundred were soused in the waters of Eaux Bonnes, Eaux Chaudes, Salies and Cambo. But although the tourists and colonists brought money into Béarn the people themselves were going through a bad patch. The railway from Bayonne to Irún had been opened and it took all the trade that hitherto, for centuries, had passed through Béarn by the Pyrenean passes. Between 1846 and 1900 nearly 30,000 Béarnais emigrated.

The foreign colony in Pau flourished again after 1870, during the rise of the Belle Epoque. The Boulevard, which runs along the edge of the town's hill and displays to its best advantage the celebrated view of the Pyrenees, was constructed.

and so were the Casino and the grand hotels between it and the Castle. The English and Scottish contingents of the new international colony introduced the noble game of Rugby football, and the Palois, fascinated, took it up themselves, which explains why Rugby, to this day, is more popular in the South-West than anywhere else in France.

The colony died at the beginning of the First World War, when everyone went home. Hideous numbers of the Béarnais died, too, as the village war memorials testify, and after the war, although tourism began to revive, the Béarnais economy did not. The opening of the Canfranc railway, up the Val d'Aspe from Oloron, helped to re-establish it, but then the Spanish civil war ruined it again.

For various reasons, which I shall come to, the Béarnais economy is pretty healthy now, which fact was evident from the dress and bearing of the busy crowds circling round Place Clémenceau. Pleasant though it may be, one cannot indulge in café-lounging for ever, and the hour of dinner would soon approach. I made my way back to the hotel, changed, then set out again, looking for a restaurant. Eventually I had to come all the way back to Place Clémenceau to an establishment about two doors away from my afternoon café, but the dinner I had there was worth the walk. Mussels were on the menu, so I had mussels; the *delicé du chef* was a small fish heavily sauced and spiced, and then there was a sort of apple pie. All this, including a half-bottle of the excellent Rosé de Béarn, came to about twenty-two and sixpence.

This excellent restaurant, which was civilized but not too grand, was called Hôtel Henri IV. 'Noustre Henric', King of France, Navarre and Béarn, is remembered in Béarn not only because he was their most notable contribution to history, but also because he personified the Béarnais way of life, which is to say that he was gay, enjoyed good food and wine, sport, and was not above a little philandering. Which is all the more remarkable because he could scarcely have had a mother who was more the antithesis of the Béarnais way of life.

A joyless, narrow-minded, Calvinistic Protestant, Queen Jeanne d'Albret had performed a signal disservice both to Christianity and to France, and her own Béarn in particular, by making Catholicism illegal in it. This brought about retribution and some bloody fighting in 1569, and the religious wars, generating a political atmosphere about as Christian as the internecine in-fighting in Imperial Rome, dragged on through the last half of the sixteenth century. By the time that Henri III of Navarre, who was the nephew of King François I of France (Marguerite d'Angoulême having been his sister) became Henri IV of France, the whole country was in a state of desperate chaos.

The chief combatants were the Protestant Huguenots and the Roman Catholic Jesuits and Gallicans. The King appealed to all the remaining moderate-minded Frenchmen sensible enough not to join the militant parties of either side, and prepared to forge together the fragments of his shattered kingdom. To begin with, he needed possession of his capital, Paris, which was in Catholic hands. As a Protestant himself, he had no hope of this; 'Paris', he observed, 'is well worth a mass.' He promised to become a Catholic and hear one, and duly at Saint-Denis he abjured Protestantism and took an oath to exterminate all heretics.

But Henri could rise above inter-Christian warfare. Having secured the support of the Catholic majority he had himself crowned in Chartres Cathedral. Then he safeguarded the lives and liberties of the Huguenots by granting them liberty of conscience and equality before the law, and made sure of this by ruling that courts of justice should be composed of elements of both factions. The Edict of Nantes guaranteed them places of unassailable refuge, one of which was La Rochelle.

The fact that he became the guardian of the puritan, Calvinistic Huguenots was somewhat incongruous when his own character is considered. He had an eye for the girls, and indulged it. One of his earlier mistresses, before he succeeded to the French throne, was one Corisande d'Andouins, a Béarnais girl from Gan, a village five miles from Pau. Corisande was not her real name (she had been reading too much romantic literature) but d'Andouins was; she came from an old and hitherto respected Béarnais family. She was pretty enough to justify her ambition of being the King's mistress, but not sufficiently intelligent to keep his affections when his royal duties took him away from Béarn, up and down the country fighting and quelling the warring factions. He transferred them (although by now married to Marguerite de Valois, whom he did not like much) to Gabrielle d'Estrées, with whom he actually lived for a while.

It was Henri's tragedy (if France's gain) that he was born into such troubled times. Surrounded on all sides by bigots, fanatics, maniacs and assassins, he had to tread a precarious path. His reputation for elusiveness sprang from the need to avoid antagonizing everyone, and the necessity, for his kingdom's good, to compromise his integrity. But among the people, the ordinary people, he acquired a popularity that still survives. He was all the things that ordinary people want in a king: he was accessible, sincere, cheerful, slightly vulgar and very far from 'holier than thou'. Also, he did his best for them; he expressed a wish that every peasant (that hitherto despised, exploited and under-nourished Jacques Bonhomme) should have 'a chicken in the pot of a Sunday'. Not just bread, which was all the peasant dared to wish for, but a chicken each, a symbol of just a little comfort and Béarnais good living. Had he lived in circumstances more like those of which his grandfather, Henri II d'Albret, made good use, perhaps he could have implemented that wish, and introduced a similar Golden Age to the benefit of the whole of France. But there were too many demented fools among his contemporaries; one of them, a fanatic called Ravaillac, assassinated him in 1610.

The busts and portraits of Henri in the castle, in the room where he was born, show him high of forehead and firm of chin (which sheltered behind a black spade beard). There is a humorous tilt to his eyebrows and an understanding (but not cynical) twinkle in his eyes.

I had originally planned to stay two nights in Pau, and make an excursion to Lescar, but I was not over-impressed by 'L'As de Trèfle' so decided to go to Lescar and stay there. The morning was quite fine and the market in Pau was in full swing when I passed it, gay with flowers and abundant vegetables and fruit, and Palois housewives engaged in a little judicial haggling. Place Grammont (Corisande d'Andouins eventually married a Grammont, a noble family who owned the castle at Bidache) was hot in the sun, and so was the busy Nationale 117, the road to Bayonne. It was also the road to

Lescar, and although walking beside a noisy, dusty and hot main road is no one's idea of heaven there was no other way. It was dead straight and passed through some rather unpleasant industrial suburbs, but at least, before the foothills hid them, one could see the Pyrenees this morning.

From the turning off the Nationale one could quite easily see Lescar, a jumble of grey and brown roofs spilling down the edge of a low ridge. Unlike many places fortified and inhabited from earliest times, such as Oloron for instance, there seemed to be no obvious reason why Lescar should have been in that particular place. The fact remains that its old name was Beneharnum, the capital of Civitas Benarnensium, and Béarnais history therefore began there.

Chapter Nine

BEARN

As I climbed the first bend of the zigzag road up the hillside to the town the rain, which had begun to threaten some half-hour since, started to fall. I passed through the main street of old houses, past the cathedral, through the ancient gateway and down the hill again. At the bottom I found Hôtel de la Terrasse, the only hotel in the town. Some boys were playing a football machine in the bar-room, and one of them, an addict, had discovered how to tilt the machine and get the balls back without putting in another coin. This he and his friends did whenever the *patronne* was not looking, which was quite often because she was the local agent for *la tiercé*, the horse-racing gamble, and had often to go and take money and issue tickets. I booked a room and waited for the rain to stop, which wasted half the afternoon because it refused to oblige until quite late. The football-machine addict, with nothing else to do, kept hanging around and fiddling about and inveigled any of his pals who dropped in to playing a game with him. He was about fourteen and had just discovered how exciting it was to swear; he did so whenever he made a false move in the game, and since he was not a very good player (despite constant practice) his small-talk involved frequent repetition, with feeling, of the word *merde*.

As soon as the weather permitted I started out to inspect the town. There is virtually no remaining evidence above ground of the original Beneharnum, because it was burnt to the ground in the ninth century by the Norman raiders, at about the same time that they similarly obliterated Illuro. It is thought that the town was resurrected, under the name of Lascarris, around the year 980, but since this was in the days when Béarnais history went by largely unrecorded no one can be quite sure. At any rate, the archaeological evidence of the tenth century is there for all to see, because quite a good deal

Gateway in Lescar

of the town's defences, and its cathedral, are still standing.

The gateway through which I now passed again closed a gap in the town walls, fragments of which have been incorporated into half the houses of the town. These consist of courses of red brick alternated with courses of rounded stones (probably from the Gave, like those used in the building of houses much later) laid in a herring-bone pattern. By the side of the gateway stands the remains of a huge tower, but judging

by a fifteenth-century-style square window in the upper part
of it, the tenth-century construction was augmented at various
later dates. The size of the tower gave the impression that the
defences must have been comprehensively complete.

In a square just the other side of the gateway stands the
cathedral. As cathedrals go, this one is not the most beautiful,
but it must be among the most aged, although, like the
defence walls, the tenth-century fabric has evidently been
added to and patched up so many times that not much of the
original is left. The walls are of a curiously assorted pattern
of red stone in a variety of shades, interspersed with red brick.
A little stunted spire caps the cruciform shape.

Inside, in pale cream stone, a colonnade of round arches
separates the barrel-vaulted nave from the aisles; the two
transepts meet in a quadripartite vault over the high altar.
Behind it, the stained-glass windows in the semi-circular
chancel are in an apparently modern cubist pattern of red,
blue, yellow and brown oblongs, and an allowance of more
windows than usual for a French cathedral makes the whole
effect much lighter.

Just inside the door I found a board naming all the bishops
of Lescar since the foundation of the see, which was simul-
taneous with the reconstruction of the town. From 1320 to
1362 I noticed that three successive bishops bore the name of
d'Andouins: ecclesiastical blood must have been running a
bit thin by the time Corisande came along.

When Béarn, by the manipulations of Viscount Gaston IV,
became attached to the Kingdom of Navarre, the cathedral of
Lescar became the family tomb of its princes; but although
the legend was strong in the town that twelve Navarrese
princes were buried there, no one knew exactly where. The
only proof was a contemporary reference which vaguely stated
that the tomb was 'before the altar of the Blessed Virgin
Mary, at the head of the choir' but there did not seem to be
any trace of it in that place or in any other. In 1929 a canon
of St Martin of Pau conducted a determined search for it,
with permission to excavate. He did so, and found the sepulchre
in the sub-soil below the main altar, after piercing a gallery
whose opening was found under the archway which separates
the left apse from the main one. Inside the tomb he found piles

of scattered bones, and among heaps of other debris, bits of
white marble mosaic, the iron parts of coffins, and pieces of a
sword. A professor of anatomy at the National Museum identi-
fied some of the bones as those of King François Phoebus (the
son, crowned at Pamplona in 1481, of Gaston IV), Prince
François de Navarre, Anne of Navarre, King Henri II
d'Albret and his Queen Marguerite d'Angoulême. For the sake

The One-Legged Moor

of the honour of Lescar, we must assume that the unidenti-
fiable remains belonged to the other seven princes. In 1933
they were all replaced in the tomb and the entrance sealed up
again.

On the floor around the main altar, at the head of the
chancel, I found the mosaic containing the Phenomenon of
the One-Legged Moor.

The mosaic is in two parts, one on either side of the altar,
and far from being ecclesiastical in character, it depicts

hunting scenes. The strip on the left of the altar has a hunter spearing a wild boar, with his dog biting its neck, and observed apparently unemotionally by a pigeon-like bird standing near. Then the picture changes the other way up so that one has to step across the mosaic to see it from the other side. Here a lion fastens on to a goat's neck while another lion looks on; and there are three more birds, one walking, one flying, and one unaccountably dead on the ground. The right-hand strip of mosaic is in the form of a procession, with a dog chained to the tail of a donkey, and both headed by this one-legged Moor, wielding a bow and arrow. As can be seen from my sketch, the stump of his deficient leg is supported by a horribly uncomfortable-looking wooden construction, but since he is striding out with considerable agility and a complacent smile on his face, it does not appear to have inconvenienced him much. Also apparent from the sketch is the information that the mosaic was made by one Bishop Guido, who from the list appears to have officiated in the early twelfth century. Any other detail about the One-Legged Moor must be guessed at. That he was a Moor is indisputable from the colour of his skin and the shape of his nose, but who was he, and how did he come to provide the good bishop with an idea for his mosaic? Maybe he was captured in one of the Crusades in Palestine or in Spain, and being treated kindly (his wound healed and the wooden attachment made for him) grew old in the bishop's service. Nobody knows, of course, but there could be a good story in it for some enterprising legend-maker. The shade of Alexandre Dumas would agree.

Outside the cathedral I wandered about the square for a while, dodging intermittent rain-showers by sheltering under huge and ancient yew trees, looking at some of the venerable houses that had been built on to even older towers, parts no doubt of the fortifications. The northern side of the square ended in a little belvedere from which the ground dropped away steeply down the hill. From its parapet I could look out over the valley of the Gave de Pau, see the soundless traffic on the Nationale 117 and the caterpillar trains, see the dark masses of the far tree-topped hills, beyond them a curtain of grey nothing, then the weird space-suspended shapes of the mountain tops, Pic d'Anie, Pic du Midi and the rest, their snowy sides gleaming orange in the faint sunlight. I stayed there, looking at them, for a long time, because it was probably the last time—a strange last time—that I should be able to see the Pyrenees on this expedition.

Hôtel de la Terrasse seemed to be rather disorganized. Madame la Patronne was mid elderly, plump, very lame in one leg, and lived from crisis to crisis. From my room while I

House in Lescar

was cleaning up before dinner I could hear her screaming abuse at the chef, and he, a tall, unshaven, unhappy (and, regrettably, rather unclean) individual, cursed back; he seemed perpetually to be on the point of walking out. A drab little woman, with the kind of countenance normally owned by gypsies of the less intelligent kind, moved about apathetically, pretending to clean things, was occasionally persuaded to serve at the bar (no one else bothered to) and was abominated and blasphemed at by both the chef, Lucien, and the *patronne*. At a point when I feared that the whole organization of the hotel (of which, as usual, I was the only resident) would disintegrate, suddenly Madame was roaring with laughter, Lucien was cooking my dinner, and the poor skivvy had gone home.

Then at last my dinner was ready; true to form, that too was unbelievably disorganized. Lucien, in his vilely filthy chef's jacket and cookhouse-check trousers, brought out each of the four courses in quick succession long before I had time to eat the last. The best thing, I found, was to eat the hot things first and leave the cold until later. It was actually well cooked, but the cold meat intended as a second course had to wait until I had finished the steak, as third. Also the whole family of the *patronne*, son-in-law, daughter and two frighteningly undisciplined little girls, were having theirs (in, I hope, less confusion than mine), making a considerable noise, and getting up and rushing about with great frequency. Both the little girls came up and gaped with jammy faces at the edge of my table and one, seeing my green tie and khaki bush-shirt (garments which usually manage to look clean longer than any other colour), asked me if I was 'a monsieur who lived in a prison?'

I was on the road to Navarrenx in good time in the morning, which was cloudy and drizzling with rain. I crossed the Nationale 117 and had just crossed the Gave de Pau when I was picked up by a man, with his daughter and dog, on their way in a small car home to Monein. The road ran beside the Gave, through a couple of small villages, until in the distance we could see chimneys and cooling towers and estates and all the paraphernalia of what the driver, a very decent man of forty or so years, called the 'industrial complex of Lacq'.

The discovery of natural gas at Lacq, after the Second World War, provided the tonic that Béarn needed. Factories were built, a new town arose at nearby Mourenx, the complex grew. By 1955 all Béarn had become buoyant, and even agriculture had been affected and rejuvenated. Aluminium and sulphur were the main products, and once more the age-old trade routes were re-established between Toulouse and Bordeaux, Bayonne and Spain; the grand design of Gaston

Phoebus for Béarn's commercial importance as the trading
centre of the South-West began once more to be realized.

We left the valley of the Gave at Arbus, climbed up into
the thickly wooded hills, emerged from a stretch of beautiful
country and stopped by a small new house. The girl and the
dog got out and went to the house. The man said: 'I'll take
you on to the other side of Monein; it'll be easier for you to
get a lift there.'

Monein is a very old town; with Jurançon, it was the earliest
wine-producing centre in Béarn. It has a twelfth-century
church, which stands in the centre of a gently sloping square
of fine Béarnais houses. Across this square we took a narrow
road and climbed a steep, winding hill, up into a misty cloud.
'If we stop here,' said the driver, 'you will be able to find the
cars which go only to Navarrenx. I will help you.'

He waited with me on the cold hill-top; there were few
cars, and all were local. We chatted, and he told me that he
had spent many years in Indo-China. 'The children, when
we returned to France, could speak more Chinese than French,
and had to start all over again at school.'

Still nothing happened, and my friend had to go home to
lunch. When he had gone I started walking along the lonely,
eerily quiet, misty road: it wound and dipped among the
fields and hills and woods, and the only habitations were
farmhouses, where ducks and chickens scratched together in
the yards and cows stood patiently in the mud. My ankles,
although still troublesome, were much better and I made
quite good progress until a fellow in a van pulled up beside
me and offered to take me the rest of the way to Navarrenx.
He was a cheerful type and chattered amiably (about nothing
in particular) all the way. Even in the murk, the prospects all
around were gladdening to the eye, of hills and woods, farms,
vineyards and pastures, some of the best I had seen in Béarn.

When we arrived in Navarrenx rain was falling steadily, so
I concluded that the best thing I could do would be to dive
into the nearest café and find something to eat. Almost at
once, having done so, I got into conversation with a little
man called M. Roger Mousquies, and there ensued a considerable politics-and-red-wine session. The referendum was
to be the next day, and M. Mousquies left me in no doubt as

to which way he would vote. 'Eleven years we have had de Gaulle, and in each successive year he becomes more and more a dictator. One dare not speak against him in public, for there are spies and informers, and if one is heard making criticisms there is likely to be a policeman near ready with the handcuffs.'

This sounded a little exaggerated to me, and I pointed out that I had seen on television the speeches of the anti-Gaullist politicians. 'Yes,' he said, 'they have had to give them an opportunity to speak. But normally there is no criticism at all on television of the Government: they run the radio services, you know. We are fast becoming a police state.'

'But surely, the fact that you are having a referendum indicates that it hasn't got as far as that yet. You are still free to vote against the General if you want to.'

'That is true; but many of us are frightened of what may happen if the General wins the referendum. Consider, Monsieur: France has been a republic since the Revolution, except for the Empire—' (and the last of the Bourbons, and Louis-Philippe, not to mention Napoleon, but never mind) '—and for a Frenchman not to feel free is intolerable. With luck the referendum will end this, and produce something new.'

'What do you think', I asked, warily, 'of the chances of the Common Market, if de Gaulle goes?'

'Oh, probably England will be admitted. But to work properly, Europe must be united, and I can't see that happening for a very long time.'

'Why?'

'Because all the nations in Europe are different, have different languages and cultures, and have been quarrelling among themselves for centuries. And yet they must unite, if they are to survive at all. Do you know what I'm afraid of most?'

'Germany?'

'No. Nor Russia. China, that's the danger. The Chinese are more dangerous than any other nation, even the Russians. I can see little hope of peace while the Chinese have the bomb.'

We had by this time disposed of the best part of a litre of wine between us, but it did not seem to incline M. Mousquies

toward optimism. Eventually he said he had to go home to
lunch and we parted; we swapped addresses and he told me
that if ever I was in Navarrenx again I was on no account to
miss visiting him. If world events go according to his prognosti-
cations, I had better make it soon, or there will not be a
chance.

After I had bought a ham sandwich and finished off the
wine, the lady of the house very kindly offered me coffee at
her expense, which helped to alleviate the uneasy feeling I
had that I was by now not entirely sober. It was still raining
when I left and made my slightly unsteady way out of the
town through a gap in its walls.

Navarrenx, in its present state, is a comparatively new
town. It originally occupied a site on the other side of the
Gave d'Oloron, but in 1523 the Prince of Orange laid siege
to and eventually completely destroyed it. My authority on
Béarnais history, M. P. Tucoo-Chala, of the Faculté des
Lettres, Bordeaux, is strangely reticent about this siege; it
took place during the admirable reign of King Henri II
d'Albret, but M. Tucoo-Chala merely observes that the King
chose Navarrenx for the building of a brand new fortress
town. Since a Prince of Orange was responsible, and Protestantism was beginning to flourish in the South of France, and
King Francis I was away on his Italian campaign against the
Emperor Charles V, one suspects that it was an opening
skirmish in the religious wars that ruined Europe in the seventeenth century.

At all events, King Henri II d'Albret, wishing to improve
his country's defences, imported an Italian military architect
from Verona, one Fabricio Siciliano. The work went on from
1542 to 1549 and the result was a new conception of defence-
walls, called *remparts élastiques* because they consisted of banks
of earth faced with stone which would absorb the iron cannon-
balls currently in use without either letting them through or
crumbling. The walls were so all-enveloping that the fortress
could be adapted to defend either Béarn, to the east, or
Basse-Navarre to the west.

An excellent opportunity for testing the Italian's theories
and King Henri's adventurous patronage of them came during
Queen Jeanne d'Albret's unfortunate reign. She, having

passed a law making Catholicism illegal in Béarn, incurred
the wrath of the King of France, Charles IX. While she was
away in La Rochelle helping the Protestant community there
in its open revolt against the King, he marched on Béarn and
besieged Navarrenx. The garrison held out to such effect that
Queen Jeanne was able to return and organize, in 1569, a
counter-attack that was entirely successful, leaving her in
possession of her Calvinistic state.

Much as the Béarnais revered their 'Grand Henric', King
Henri IV, their Protestant leaders of the day do not seem to
have learned from his policy of tolerance and forbearance in
religious matters. By 1620 they had become so impertinent
that Henri's son, King Louis XIII, who had none of his
father's affection for Béarn, led an army there to such effect
that the intransigent Protestants were firmly squashed and
Catholicism was officially reinstated. The new church, of
Saint-Germain, which had been built in the new Navarrenx
only seventy-odd years before, was re-consecrated in the
Catholic faith, and furthermore Basse-Navarre and Béarn were
quite definitely attached to France, losing their independence.

I crossed the old bridge over the Gave and took the road to
Sauveterre, on which, after a while, I was picked up by a
bespectacled, intelligent young lady in one of those desperately
insubstantial little two-horse Citroëns. The road ran along
the top of the hills besides the Gave valley. At the crossroads
leading to Sauveterre we parted and I trotted down through
the dreary gloom of the sadly moist afternoon to a town that
looked far more of a fortress than Navarrenx. It stood on a
high ridge which projected into a bend in the river (a favourite
site for castle-builders) and looked like a series of castles, so
numerous, although a bit run-down, were its towers. I crossed
the brown, swirling and dangerously high Gave again and
climbed up to the town. I started looking for hotels, of which
there were several, and first tried one in the square. It was
now pouring down and everyone in the town seemed to be
sheltering in this bar, all wearing their berets, drinking red
wine and talking hard—tomorrow's referendum provided an
inexhaustible topic. I liked the look of the place, because it
was an old house with a fine staircase and this room full of
Sauveterre citizens had such a gloriously local atmosphere,

but they had no rooms to let. Nor had the second place I tried, but for a different reason: the bar was empty, and they were not beginning their hotel operations until the season was under way. I finished up at a place which I had passed by earlier because it displayed one of those enamelled plaques saying 'Hôtel de Tourisme' which I knew for a certainty meant thirty francs a night (I was quite correct) but every minute I stayed out meant getting still wetter.

I had to admit that 'A Boste', Auberge Béarnaise, was a fascinating place in which to stay, because the staircase up to the bedrooms was stone, and spiral, and turned out to be a turret of the Sauveterre castellation system. This was rather complicated, as I have intimated, because it had been amended and strengthened at several different times by several different military architects.

The oldest parts of the castle are relics of the eleventh century and were probably raised by order of one of the early viscounts (perhaps Centulle V; he was enterprising enough to revive Oloron, so he could have organized the defences of so obviously important a stronghold as Sauveterre). Then came a strengthening addition of ramparts and walls by Viscount Gaston VII Moncade, builder of Tour Moncade in Orthez in the thirteenth century, and further amendments by Viscount Gaston Phoebus, as part of his overall scheme of improving Béarnais defences in the fourteenth.

The earlier importance of its strategic position, as a bastion of Béarn (perhaps hence its name) was mainly relevant to possible attacks from the Basques, who appear to have been inordinately aggressive in those years, as is evident from their treatment of Charlemagne's rearguard at Roncesvalles. The last time they attacked Sauveterre was in the sixteenth century, after an earlier siege by the same Prince of Orange who laid waste Navarrenx. M. Tucoo-Chala is not too forth-coming about that, either.

The result of the successive castle-builders, and the battered remains of their efforts following the sieges, is that everywhere one goes in Sauveterre one finds bits of castle. If one's house did not include part of a section of castle, it would be un-usual. Even the church, which arose during the thirteenth century, Gaston VII Moncade's era, has a huge stone tower and looks like part of it, too. The fortifications are massive and must have been an impressive deterrent even to the bellicose Basques.

The cooking 'A Boste', Auberge Béarnaise, was very good, without being exceptional, but the atmosphere in the dining-room, which I shared with three other single men, was arctic. No one spoke or even smiled, and three thin cats roamed from one to another, staring and importuning with huge accusing eyes and very little charm of manner.

The morning was drier but still overcast. After a stroll round Sauveterre inspecting the ramparts and the omni-present castle-parts (the one attached to the hotel, the stair-case, was slippery and I very nearly cascaded down it—I was two floors up as usual) I set off back down the hill to the bridge across the surging Gave. The salmon-fishing season was then on, and championships were advertised on colourful posters all over the place. The Gave d'Oloron is apparently a very good salmon river, and catches reach remarkable pro-portions. Judging by the low-lying fields on either side of the Gave, the river must have been much wider in earlier centuries, probably lapping the lower castle walls.

I climbed back up to the crossroads and took the road to Bayonne. It was not long before I was offered transport there by a young lady who wanted to be in Bayonne half an hour ago; she travelled at the speed of light over roads which had clearly not been made up since Gaston Phoebus, and before long my interior, in a delicate state anyway after the red-wine session in Navarrenx, began to feel like an instant whip. When we passed (overtaking Graham Hill and a VC 10 on the way) by the foot of Labastide Villefranche, I was still able to notice the Donjon used as a fronton and the baroque excesses of 'Le Bijou'; by Peyrehorade the confluence of the Gaves d'Oloron and de Pau, and the nice little square castle might have been on another planet. At this point I asked if I might open the window, to let in some air; also at this point we joined the Nationale 117 and from there until we zoomed into Bayonne the working parts of my anatomy were always a kilometre or two behind.

We came to a halt in Place de la République and the young lady, imperturbable to the last, glanced at her watch. She was only twenty minutes late for her appointment, which should have been at eleven o'clock: the time when she picked me up outside Sauveterre had been 10.40, and the distance from there to Bayonne was sixty kilometres—about thirty-seven miles.

Chapter Ten

BAYONNE

I sat on a bench in Place de la République for a full twenty
minutes, breathing deeply, feeling my senses returning and my
internal arrangements gradually unscrambling themselves. The
quarter of Saint-Esprit, into which I had been thrust, was
across the river from the city of Bayonne; it was hemmed in
by the grassy hills, on top of which was a huge fortress, called
la Citadelle, designed by Vauban and garrisoned by Soult's
men in 1813 when Wellington was advancing from Spain. At
the bottom of this hill was the railway station, a little church
and Place de la République. Around the Place were a number
of hotels: I picked one called Hôtel Saint-Esprit. It looked
quite modern from the front, but inside was vast, with a
massive wooden staircase that seemed to go on up for ever,
like the Tower of Babel. My room, naturally, was two floors up.

After a sandwich and a beer at a café facing the station and
called Etche Ona (Good House—a favourite title among
Basque hotels and cafés), I crossed the bridge over the wide
Adour to the city of Bayonne.

One cannot say that Bayonne is a Basque city, despite its
name, for it is as much a Landais, Béarnais and Gascon
capital. The Tarbelli, the westernmost of the Nine Peoples
who inhabited the coastal plains, the Landes, and the lower
Adour and Garonne valleys, were the first to build it, and its
old name was Lapurdum. With the passing of the centuries
and the evolution of the Gascons, who may or may not have
been 'Basques who spoke Latin' the city, although belonging
to the dukes of Aquitaine (which was another name for
Gascony), obtained the charter of a free town about the year
1120 and took its name from the Euskara words Baï-ona,
which means Good River.

This same river, the Adour, and the roads which run beside
it, introduced the Béarnais element, for, although many miles

138

Bayonne

from Bèarn, Bayonne has always handled much of Béarn's produce. Nowadays this consists mostly of the sulphur, aluminium and phosphates of the Lacq complex, all of which can be transported easily to Bayonne and exported by sea.

There are actually two rivers at Bayonne, but the Nive, which empties into the Adour a little way upriver from the bridge, is nothing like as long or wide. I last came across it at Saint-Jean Pied-de-Port.

On the tongue of land between the two rivers there is a garden and the statue of a bishop. Just across the second bridge, and facing the riverside, the Municipal Theatre stands in splendid isolation. This is a huge, well-proportioned, rectangular building, with arcades all around and ground-floor space occupied by shops and cafés. It was at present showing films, all of which seemed to be about either M. Maigret or Ruritanian princesses.

A fine, wide boulevard with trees and grand shops led up the very slight rise of Bayonne's hill, past the old castle, to the cathedral, whose twin spires over the west porch can be seen for miles. The cathedral was built in the latter part of the thirteenth century to replace a Romanesque basilica burnt down in 1258; but that too had to be rebuilt after another fire, in 1310. The style chosen was Gothic, and the spires were added in the nineteenth century. Looking up at them it is easy to see where the new work starts because the stone changes colour. The old stone, a warm yellow, has been terribly eroded by time and the elements, but the work of restoring it is already half-way through; one side of the porch looks like London after the blitz, the other is crisp, clean and pure of line, as if brand new. It has been beautifully done.

The interior of the cathedral was dark, because the after-noon was still uncompromisingly overcast. But the windows were tall and full of some beautiful stained glass, and as my eyes became more accustomed to the gloom I could see the tall graceful pillars reaching up into the roof of the nave, splaying and spreading out like the branches of trees, and where the branches crossed, one side meeting the other, were bosses decorated with coloured coats of arms. One of these, faintly visible in the dim light, showed three golden crouching leopards, one above another, on red: the arms of the Kings of England.

If one thinks about this, the incidence of an English royal coat of arms in a French cathedral is not as surprising as it might at first seem. At the time of the second fire, when the roof would have been finally completed, the King of England was Edward III and it was during his long reign that his family's claim on their French dominions was upheld and firmly established. Bayonne was among them.

After fifteen years of fruitless marriage King Louis VII of France and his Queen Eleanor discovered, conveniently, that they were cousins and should never have been married in the first place. Their marriage was annulled and two months later Eleanor married Henry of Anjou, a very young man (of twenty-one: she was thirty-ish) who four months after that succeeded to the crown of England. Now Henry already possessed Normandy, Brittany, Maine and Anjou, and it just so happened that Eleanor was heiress of Poitou, and Aquitaine, which included Guyenne and Gascony, the Basque Country and Béarn. King Henry II of England therefore found himself in command of an empire which stretched from the Tweed to the Pyrenees, and included more French land than the King of France himself possessed.

But it never functioned as an empire, because there was never any feeling of identity with one nation, or unity. The diplomatic ineptitude of King John lost him Anjou, Brittany, Normandy and Maine, but Aquitaine remained loyal to its Duke, the King of England. Trade with England—the old Béarnais precept of neutrality bringing prosperity—was extremely profitable, and no Gascon thought himself either French or English. Those were the feudal ages and one simply acknowledged one's liege lord, whoever he was.

When the French royal family of Capet became extinct King Edward III of England claimed the throne because he was a Capet nephew, and thought he had a good chance of regaining his old territories and more besides. The crown went to a cousin, Philip of Valois, and Edward went to war. He adventured very successfully from 1346 to 1347, beat Philip and regained much of the lost ground. Ten years later his son, the Black Prince, operating from Bordeaux, beat Philip's successor John (called the Good: he was a good man, but the same could not be said of his abilities as a soldier), captured him at Poitiers, and tacked Poitou on to Aquitaine. For twenty years the Black Prince ruled the South-West of France, and on the whole its inhabitants do not seem to hold it against him: he was their Duke, and he kept the peace, which enabled them to conduct their businesses regularly and get rich and fat.

But Bertrand du Guesclin rose to prominence; in 1376 the Black Prince died, and the King his father in the following year. By that time, also, France had a king, Charles V, who was a tactician. He did not engage in pitched battles with the English, because he knew they generally won them (he was called 'the Wise'), but waged a war of perpetual and irritating nagging, which was much more effective, and gradually recovered his territories.

From then on, except for the meteoric reign of Henry V, who revived Edward III's original claims and emphasized them forcefully at Agincourt, the English possessions dwindled. Gascony remained loyal because business was still good, and even Joan of Arc failed to excite them very much in the South-West. Even Gascony, however, had to yield to increasing French pressure and increased confidence. England's last soldier, Talbot, Earl of Shrewsbury, was killed at Castillon (the battle at Bidache must have been about this time) in 1453, and English rule in the fair land of France came to an end.

The Gascons, as it turned out, were perfectly justified in their loyalty to the English kings, because as soon as they departed their new rulers treated them very harshly, fouled up their commercial arrangements, taxed them and oppressed them, and not unnaturally incurred the Gascons' whole-hearted resentment.

At all events, they have left the arms of England on that boss in the cathedral of Bayonne; and perhaps a little of the old affiliation was left in their minds when Wellington came to chase out Napoleon's armies, and they actively welcomed him.

While I was in the cathedral, looking at the leopards, the stained glass and the awesome beauty of the soaring columns, a boy and his tutor were practising the organ; not the great organ over the porch but a small electric one near the altar. They were still at it when I left to look at the cloisters on the south side. These were built at the same time as the cathedral, round all four sides of a green: cool, graceful, tranquil.

I wandered through narrow streets of tall old houses, many in the deep-eaved, timbered Basque style, until I reached the city wall, several of the towers of which had been incorporated, like the bits of castle in Sauveterre, into houses and hotels. I crossed the Nive and walked along its banks, where the houses had arcades along their fronts in the same style I had seen in so many Basque towns and villages. Those in Bayonne, called *Arceaux*, were reputedly once the haunt of pirates (presumably in the days when that noble profession was popular among the Basque sailors, the fishing industry having gone to pot) and are still a meeting place for sailors and fishermen.

Just past another bridge over the Nive (which was that day a repulsive colour like tea with too much milk in it) I found the huge old stone house which accommodates the Basque Museum. It was closed (the day was Sunday) so I resolved to come back the next morning, first thing. I had visited it before, but that was more than four years earlier and one forgets things.

I went into one of the bars in the *Arceaux*, expecting an atmosphere of fish, tar, sailors' tales and plug tobacco, but everyone was watching a tennis match on television and admiring a perfectly appalling little dog owned by the *patronne*. I was disappointed, but the tennis match was a good one.

My hotel's restaurant was not yet open, so I went to one just along the road, still in Place de la République, called Hôtel Côte Basque. Here I had a thoroughly Basque meal, starting with fish soup, which although not so designated on the menu was presumably something like a Basque dish called *Ttoro*. Next came another Basque speciality called *Piperade*, an omelette with tomatoes and green peppers. The recipes for these dishes vary somewhat (a characteristic of all genuinely national country dishes: no one's granny cooks them in exactly the same way as someone else's) but can be found in most international cookery books, such as Elizabeth David's *French Provincial Cooking*. The Piperade in particular I found excellent. The bill, with dessert and a half litre of wine, came to less than a pound.

At breakfast I asked the very helpful man at my hotel how yesterday's referendum had gone, but the results had only just started to come in. Rain was spattering dismally down in that infuriatingly persistent way that had recurred so often during these travels—'It is not', I was told quite earnestly and fre- quently, 'at all normal for this time of year.' By the time I had visited the nearest bank for money and the post office for letters I was considerably wet, so the rest of the morning spent in the Musée Basque seemed a sensible idea. In point of fact I should have gone in the afternoon, because I forgot what time it was, and when I had spent twenty minutes inspecting the fascinating things in the first room, one of the caretakers cheerfully reminded me that there were forty others and all would close at mid-day.

I hurried round to see and take in as much as possible, but it was the kind of place in which one could wander all day. The building in which it is housed (I change to the present tense but the future would seem more appropriate) is a vast, massively solid old merchant's house, built round a triangular courtyard. It is several storeys high, mainly of stone but incorporating so much wood that it is no wonder that there is no longer an oak forest in the valley of Hasparren. The staircase, all of oak, would support an elephant, and the floor-boards and doors would rebuild Nelson's navy. It is four or five hundred years old and is clearly still in its infancy.

Its contents could provide anyone interested in the Basques was a comprehensive knowledge of them, of their origins, history, habits and customs, achievements, culture, and virtually anything else about them. There are pictures of people in their traditional dress, life-sized models wearing it, whole rooms set out as they still are in houses with big canopied beds, kitchens full of copper and brass pots and pans, ornamental candlesticks, carved wooden tables, chairs, benches and cradles; there is a room devoted entirely to the national sport, pelota, and all its offshoots, models of players in the requisite white shirt and trousers, red belt and red or blue beret, cases full of examples of the *chistera* and rackets for the variation called *sare*, balls in sections to show how they are made, photographs of champion players. One of these was Chiquito of Cambo, an all-time superlative, who is supposed once to have won a match of paleta, playing with a champagne bottle; a parallel would be W. G. Grace having scored a century with a broomstick.

Two items in particular drew my attention. One was a case full of relics of the Basque regiments which participated in the Spanish Carlist wars of the nineteenth century. The Basques seem to have had the unfortunate tendency to back the wrong side in Spanish disputes: in both the Carlist wars, 1833–9 and 1872–6, the Basques fought for the Pretender and his son. The King held his own, and as a result the Spanish Basques lost the last of their freedoms, exemption from military service. In 1936, when Spain became briefly a republic, the Basques were granted full autonomy (in the Museum are flags, coins, bank-notes, issued in this brief era of freedom). Therefore they took the Republicans' part in the Civil War, and have consequently been part of Spain again, ever since.

The other point I will mention was a room full of details, and specimens, of the manufacture of the *makhila*. This is the traditional swagger-cane of the Basques, and is supposed to have a sharp point cunningly sheathed inside, to add force to the swagger. It is made of polished wood, at the top a handle of plaited leather with a loop (like a riding-whip) and a horn button at the end, at the bottom an engraved brass tip (concealing the sharp point). The only *makhila*-makers now existing (they have the monopoly) are at Larressore, near Espelette. The family of Aïnciart-Bergara holds the hereditary secret of how to tint the medlar-wood used in the shaft, and turns out about three hundred a year. Most of these, one suspects, are sold as souvenirs to tourists, since even on a Sunday I never saw a Basque holding one. There was, however, beneath a row of types of *makhila* in the museum room, a long poem in Euskara, with a translation in French, about their manufacture. Here is the first verse, with a translation (regrettably a little rough, I fear) of the translation:

'Horra non den makhila,   'There it is, the makhila,
  Gan guzian atzarririk,   Up all night to make it,
  Phartitzeko chutiturik.'   It stands there, ready to go.'

The *makhila* is one of the ancient habitual adjuncts of the Basques which seem to have become dispensable in the late twentieth century. Henry Myhill says that one can 'always recognize a Basque when one sees one. And this is not only because of his characteristic physiognomy'. A Basque, he maintains, always wears a blue beret (or possibly red—a relic of the Carlist attachment) and invariably a white shirt. The Basques I saw during my travels in their country certainly wore berets, but then so does most of the rest of France. The *beret Basque*, moreover, is made exclusively in Béarn. Of the white shirt I saw little. French *ouvrier* blue overalls predominated. It would seem, then, that while Euzkadi Bat is still as important as ever, and Euskara is being vigorously maintained by Spanish if not French Basques, the traditional forms of dress even in the most simplified form have been abandoned except, probably, for festivals and feasts. And might one perhaps venture to suggest, only then for the benefit of tourists? At the wedding in Santesteban, an event one would have thought eminently suitable for the production and wear of best indigenous garb, everyone was in white shirts admittedly, but they were worn with snappy twentieth-century gents' natty suiting; and among the girls not one example of red, green or blue, white-embroidered *linge Basque* was to be seen.

I managed to see most of the other forty rooms in the museum before the amiable little caretaker (who was certainly wearing his blue beret, indoors, whether or not it was made in Oloron) came trotting up flourishing his keys. Since I was the only visitor that morning you could hardly blame him for wanting to hurry and lock up and go to lunch.

It was still drizzling intermittently, but not so heavily, so I wandered off to look at the Château Neuf and the nearby church of Saint-André. Both castles, new and old, were planned and re-planned respectively by the ubiquitous Vauban, in the seventeenth century. They are both still military depots, with garrisons at present from the Parachute Corps of France, a crack regiment with an appropriately smart uniform. The soldiers wear a red beret of a shade similar to our equivalent, with the badge over the left ear and the right side pulled well down; vast quantities of coloured cords are worn draped over the left shoulder, and there is clearly a considerable *esprit de corps*. I several times encountered soldiers tramping about the streets of Bayonne, off duty, stamping their feet gaily and singing *Lily the Pink* with Rugby-club gusto.

The Château Neuf used for decades to be the depôt of the 49th Infantry Regiment (whose proud record was illustrated in the Museum). A plaque at the gateway to the castle says that the regiment distinguished itself in the First World War by losing 2,840 casualties; if the regiment was recruited from the South-West, this accounts for the tragically long lists of names on the war memorials of even the smallest villages.

The Château Vieux, in the street leading up to the cathedral, although redesigned by Vauban, was built when Bayonne was Lapurdum as a Roman fortress, and has been rebuilt by successive viscounts and governors over the years. It too has a plaque outside, recording the latter fact and listing the important personages who have stayed in it. These include several of the leading characters in the stories told in these pages:

'Don Alonso the Warrior, King of Navarre (1130); the Black Prince; du Guesclin and Don Pedro the Cruel, King of Castille (1367); King Louis XI' (who granted the privileges to Saint-Jean-de-Luz, '(1463); King François I' (on his way home after being exchanged for his children at the Island of Pheasants), '(1526); King Charles IX' (anti-Protestant operations), '(1565); King Louis XIV' (more privileges for Saint-Jean-de-Luz), '(1660); Marie-Anne de Neuborg, Queen of Spain (1706); and General Palafox (1809).'

The date, 1367, quoted for the Black Prince's sojourn at the castle was during his reign as Duke of Gascony, after the fighting was over. But an English army (without him, admittedly) landed in Bayonne in 1345, and since it embarked on three campaigns, designed as diversions for King Edward III's operations at Crécy, which are far less known than the latter battle, perhaps a brief account of them would be of interest.

The army, consisting of 500 men-at-arms and 2,000 archers, under the command of Henry of Lancaster, then Earl of Derby, disembarked at Bayonne in June 1345. The three campaigns which it fought were designed first, as previously remarked, to cover the King's expedition, and secondly to reconquer his territories from the French king. All three campaigns were completely successful: the first, on the Dordogne, covered Bordeaux from possible threats from Paris, and regained the Périgord district. The second, on the Garonne, safeguarded the Périgord from possible attack from Toulouse; the third recovered Saintonge and most of Poitou.

Most of us connect English military operations in France in the fourteenth century with the King and the Black Prince; the forgotten man is Henry of Lancaster, who conducted and commanded all those brilliant operations and also seems to have been a man of irreproachable character. The best praise is that which comes from the other side. The French historian Henri Bertrandy said: 'These campaigns have imprinted upon the memory of Derby an indestructible glory. This illustrious Englishman displayed all the qualities which in their entirety form the appanage of the truly great.'

These qualities, rare enough in anyone, rarer still in military commanders, were succinctly categorized by Sir Winston Churchill, who possessed them in the highest degree: 'In War: Resolution. In Defeat: Defiance. In Victory: Magnanimity. In Peace: Goodwill.'

The English army during these campaigns, which were fought to free the English crown from the vassalage of the French crown and to re-establish its claim to possessions on French soil, reached the heights of professional quality. The King seems to have had that quality of leadership which inspires absolute loyalty, and furthermore he was extremely lucky in his lieutenants, of whom Derby was one. They worked together with mutual respect and understanding, were never guilty of jealousy and never quarrelled, and were all highly competent. Any army reflects its leaders, and the King's armies responded fully to their inspiring leadership. The long bow during this period was developed into the most deadly and effective weapon the army possessed until the Lee-Enfield rifle.

I went for lunch to another café in Place de la République and had some ham. Bayonne is famous for ham, and for chocolate which has been made there for two hundred years. It is also famous for the invention of the bayonet, a less agreeable article. It inspired one poet (Tristan Derème), evidently crossed in love like all good poets, to write these lines, which do not need translating:

'L'oeil de la Bayonnaise est une baïonette,
        Adour, cruel Adour, quand tu nous tiens!'

I went to the city in the afternoon, bought a newspaper, sat in one of the cafés on the ground floor of the Municipal Theatre and read about the referendum. The 'Noes' had it; the General, defeated, had resigned. But there was no fervour:

no thronging the streets, shouting and singing, no shots, barricades, chaos. Everyone was taking it very calmly, talking about it, certainly, discussing it among themselves, but not allowing themselves to get excited. One reason, I discovered from the newspaper, was that the South-West as a whole had voted '*Oui*' (doubtless with the exception of M. Mousquies of Navarrenx), and the difference in any case was very slight. No one seemed quite to know what would happen next, except that M. Poher, the President of the Assembly, would assume the national presidency until an election could be held.

I did some shopping, returned to Saint-Esprit, packed and made ready to leave by the evening train. I called in at Hôtel Etche Ona for a last couple of red wines, asked Madame, a young-middle-aged lady, to make me up a sandwich for the journey, and then asked her opinion of the referendum result.

'I suppose', I suggested, 'that there will be many changes in policy now, and most people will be glad of a new government.'

'Yes,' she said, not enthusiastically, 'possibly things ought to change. But after all, you know, he was a man of honour, and he did a great deal for France. Not, perhaps, so much for the people materially, but a lot for our rise in the eyes of the world. From a laughing-stock, with a new government every other month, he brought us to a state of self-respect and pride. It seems a shame that he should go this way.'

'Who will be next? Poher?'

'No, I doubt it. He's all right, but we don't know much about him. I hope, Pompidou.'

I crossed the square to the station to join the soldiers waiting for the train, and wondered why we could not have a referendum or two at home.

BIBLIOGRAPHY

BELLOC, HILAIRE: *The Pyrenees*, 1909.
BORROW, GEORGE: *The Bible in Spain*, 1843.
BURNE, LT.-COL. ALFRED H.: *The Crécy War*, 1955.
DEANESLY, MARGARET: *A History of Early Mediaeval Europe, 476–911*, 1956.
DUMAS, ALEXANDRE: *The Three Musketeers*, 8 vols., 1844.
EPTON, NINA: *Navarre*, 1957.
GLOVER, MICHAEL: *Wellington's Peninsular Victories*, 1963.
GUERARD, ALBERT: *France*, 1959.
MYHILL, HENRY: *The Spanish Pyrenees*, 1966.
O'CONNELL, D. P.: *Richelieu*, 1968.
SNEATH, GUY: *The Basque Country*, 1966.
TUCOO-CHALA, P.: *Histoire de Béarn*, 1962.
YATES, DORNFORD: *Jonah & Co.*, 1922.

INDEX